Children Who Could Have Been

William M. Epstein

Children Who Could Have Been

The Legacy of Child Welfare in Wealthy America

The University of Wisconsin Press

The University of Wisconsin Press
2537 Daniels Street
Madison, Wisconsin 53718

3 Henrietta Street
London WC2E 8LU, England

From *The Mask* by Dean Koontz (pp. 6–7). Copyright © by Nkui, Inc.
Used by permission of Putnam Berkley, a division of Penguin Putnam Inc.

Library of Congress Cataloging-in-Publication Data
Epstein, William M., 1944–
    Children who could have been : the legacy of child welfare in wealthy
America / by William Epstein.
    176 pp.   cm.
    Includes bibliographical references and index.
    ISBN 0-299-16380-6 (cloth: alk. paper)
    1. Child welfare—United States.   I. Title.
HV741.E67   1999
362.7′0973—dc21   99-13086

You don't understand. I coulda had class. I coulda been a contender. I coulda been somebody.

Terry Malloy in On the Waterfront, *1954*

Contents

Acknowledgments

I am grateful to many people for assistance and advice. Gerald Hardcastle, a remarkable family court judge, sparked my early interest in this project. Natalie and Adam were patient, enduring my questions and recalling very painful events. The Boys Town staff—Pookie and Jeff Hopgood, Holly and Mike Skofield, Tom Waite—were frank and encouraging; without any assurance of congenial findings, the organization in both Las Vegas and Omaha was still helpful and forthcoming. The faculty of Cheyenne High School and numerous therapists, counselors, social workers, and child care workers (unnamed to preserve the identities of Natalie and Adam) provided important information. Many of the students at the School of Social Work, University of Nevada, Las Vegas, with years of experience in public child care, shared their experiences. The Department of Child and Family Services of the State of Nevada—Janell Ahlvers, Stuart Fredlund, Maria Grant, Marie Myles, and Annette Simmons—assisted enormously; there are many hardworking, intelligent, committed, and skilled public servants who have been unfairly burdened by the mindless antagonism of recent politics toward public service. Two psychiatrists—Norton Roitman and my brother, Paul Epstein—have opened doors into the souls of maltreated children. Numerous reviewers have improved the content and the text: Marvin Bloom, Carol Case, Robert Dippner, Ronald Farrell, Stuart Fredlund, Robert Morris, Steve Nielson, Thom Reilly, Jerry Rubin, Linda Santangelo, and David Stoesz. My research assistant, Jennifer Duddy, is in a class by herself. The staff of the library at the University of Nevada, Las Vegas, provided exceptional service. Denise DiMaggio toiled over the index.

In addition to individuals, I am grateful for academic tenure, which frees the consideration of embedded institutions and powerful actors from toiling under a social boss.

Introduction

Something wonderful has happened in the United States, but it is not the public system of child welfare services. The wealth and freedoms of this astonishingly multiethnic, multiracial, intellectually diverse, and culturally rich nation are an envied model for global development. However, the nation's meager response to its own children who must rely on public generosity suggests that neither its successes nor its sacrifices are shared fairly. The issues of deservingness and blame do not impinge on children, at least in the rhetoric and social dialectics of welfare. In contrast with adult recipients of public welfare, children without parents obviously deserve care; their claims to relief and protection are unimpeachable. Innocent of social or spiritual corruption, they are not morally responsible for the failures of their parents.

Public child welfare services include the surveillance system for children—protective services—that customarily provides entry to care. Yet the largest portion of the system is devoted to custodial arrangements for children, notably including foster care (with families and in congregate settings) but also including adoption services, treatment centers, and shelters. In 1995, the public child welfare system provided care for more than 700,000 children and touched the lives of many hundreds of thousands more through investigations of complaints and through interventions designed to prevent placement.

The meaning of the public child welfare system obviously lies in its provisions for children who are neglected, abused, or abandoned, but, more important, the system of care expresses a collective state of mind. The services themselves realize particular social goals, values, moods, and attitudes. Indeed, the problems of the public child welfare system stem from the society's collective refusal to provide adequately for children who must rely on the goodwill of the American people.

The poverty of the public response to these children's needs opens windows into the nation's soul, testing the sincerity of its civic philosophy. It fails the test badly, exposing itself as hypocritical if not actually cynical. Indeed, the public child welfare system is evidence of a profound disregard by most of the nation's citizens for many of their fellow citizens.

This is not a novel observation. However, the growing inequality in the United States occurs along with a large growth in its wealth, its increased capacity to handle its problems. What is remarkable is the broad and stubborn refusal to do so.

The decision to neglect blameless and dependent children is profoundly political. It did not occur accidentally, and the system's policies were not developed naively. The austerity of the child welfare system is not the result of any national emergency or even the cunning victory of conservatism. Rather, contemporary American social welfare policy is the result of an esurient, pernicious liberalism that has led the national capitulation to public irresponsibility. The conservative impulse in the United States, especially as it affects social welfare, has been consistently savage, led by the plangent and plaintive cry of the coddled businessman for greater profits and more secure conditions under which to pursue them. Conservatives have fashioned a policy of public neglect under the convenient banner of social Darwinism and through a Puritan sense of personal responsibility for characterological imperfection.

Conservatism has been a rock of cruelty over the years. Its posturing intellectuals and sibilant aristocrats—Buckley, Murray, Herrnstein, Meade, Kristol, Podhoretz—and its more strident ideologues—Gilder, Rushton, Jensen, Shockley—have convinced a receptive liberal ear that less is more. The stern necessity of a stark public provision has become a broadly popular strategy of acculturation. Less public education, less sharing in the nation's comforts, less security for workers, less training and opportunity for those who wish to work, less medical coverage, less public housing, less for those who cannot work or are too impaired to work, and even less protection for the most blameless. Obviously, less public social welfare implies less in taxes.

The most rebarbative impulses of conservatism have been muted over the years by a natural political opposition among the poor, the marginalized, the unsuccessful, the immigrant, and the disaffected. The balance of power between the conservative community and its natural opposition has been controlled by a liberal voice speaking both to a managerial middle class and to a mobile working class. As the middle class has suffered economically and socially and as its perceived freedoms and status have become threatened, it has traditionally sought refuge in an empowered public sector.

Perhaps the startling wealth of the United States has purchased the liberal's acquiescence with the supremacy of economic growth as the nation's supreme social value. The liberal voice has been speaking in a conservative language for decades, undermining historic protections for workers, dampening unionism, providing tax expenditures for the wealthiest, and abandoning the protections of the public sector. With a convert's intensity, liberalism has blinded its critical capacities with the belief that the behemoth of business has matured into a Paul Bunyan of social virtue.

For their own security, liberals have backed into vapidity—a tepid structuralism that denies the gravity of need and that offers only a patina of concrete services and superficial, ineffective procedural reforms. The withering away of the progressive impulse in America has handed political influence to a variety of conservatives—most prominently, the religious right and commercial interests—along with the marching and chowder society liberals. The opposition is ineffective, largely composed of people so hampered by their own problems as to obviate effective political participation and their camp following of quaint intellectual bohemians.

The drift toward a pernicious liberalism has been facilitated by the social welfare literature itself. The intellectuals in the human services research and development industry, mainly residing in academia and most frequently considering themselves to be liberals if not actually social radicals, have rationalized public neglect.[1] They have failed to introduce a voice of objectivity and neutrality into policy discourse. Rather, human service intellectuals, influenced by the popular orthodoxy of American politics, have produced compliant evidence for a parsimonious social welfare response to children dependent on public care. Their many departures from accepted social science practice have consistently provided bogus evidence for a policy of social efficiency—that meagerly funded, superficial, and socially compatible service programs can achieve important social goals. When not actually full-gospel testimonials to success, the research claims

1. Human services, social services, personal social services, social work services, and so forth, are used throughout as nearly synonymous. They are not meant to include medical care, public health services, and education. They refer to the remaining and enormous range of services that have the goal of cure, prevention, and rehabilitation of people suffering from personal or social problems. They include psychotherapeutic as well as such material services as day care, respite care, health care, cash assistance, food stamps, and housing. As such they focus on mental health, social adjustment, personal adaptation, vocational and skills training (but not basic or professional education). Within these constraints, human service is used as the broadest term and may connote some aspiration for universality, whereas social services have a narrower meaning, focusing on personal adaptation usually through some sort of agency-based delivery of specific interventions. Social work services refer to those services provided specifically by social workers with degrees in the field. Admittedly, the differences are small and frequently the terms are used interchangeably to provide some variation and to mirror the context of the literature.

to identify hopeful leads to future effectiveness, in the manner of bread mold killing bacteria in a petri dish.

Dissent in personal service research is raised by a rare and atrophic arm. The accommodations of the community of personal service researchers are organizationally comprehensible. Pressures to affirm the nation's enchantment with social efficiency operate powerfully through the incentives and penalties exercised by government as well as by the private sector: on the one hand, research and service funding, social status and prestige, and professional advancement; on the other hand, budget cuts and obscurity.

The human service research is evidence of the processes of accommodation and justification by which child welfare policy is created. The role that human service professionals and intellectuals act out in the play of power departs from their own grandiose advertisement of nobility, advocacy, and service; the child welfare system provides little welfare. Seemingly inspired by the Poor Law principle of less eligibility, the American child welfare system ensures that working-class and poor children will have working-class and poor futures into which to carry their emotional, mental, physical, and social deficits.

Any sensible field should have learned modesty after so many decades during which programmatic failure has been the only constant. However, the human service professions trumpet notable successes, paths to insight, indications of progress, and hopeful leads like a devilish five year old banging pot covers together to announce the opening of her tree house.

The issue of authority lies at the center of the policy-making process. Impelled by ambition to emulate the social status of medicine and engineering, the human services have embraced science to achieve rational credibility for professional knowledge. Scholarship in the human services must ultimately focus on the effectiveness of particular social and public policies—specific child welfare programs. In turn, claims for effective service outcomes carry authority to the extent to which they are founded on research that utilizes rational, that is, scientific, methodologies.

The application of science to the human services confronts a unique set of problems notably because its objects of inquiry, people, presumably exercise independent wills and are active, conscious subjects in the research process. The assumption that the objects of study in the hard sciences lack motive and consciousness, justifiable perhaps for the physicist's scrutiny of quarks, does not transfer well to fields that study people. Human research must be methodologically sensitive to potential biases of subjects, researchers, and research situations that can undermine claims for the effectiveness of the service interventions—that is, they must certify that the services and the services alone caused the outcomes.

Rational research in the human services—the task of testing the causal relationship between services and outcomes—entails the use of randomized controlled trials (RCTs) along with other methodological protections of science (Epstein 1993b; Fleiss 1986; Meinert 1986). Fully implemented RCTs employ prospective experimentation, random selection of subjects from an underlying population of need and random assignment to experimental and control groups, placebo or at least nontreatment or standard treatment control conditions, objective, reliable measurement, follow-up measurement, blinding, and other safeguards to ensure the scientific credibility of research.

RCTs are expensive, inconvenient, frequently impractical, and under certain circumstances, both illegal and immoral. The nation cannot be given two governments or two economies; subjects cannot be deprived of traditional protections of law; children cannot be arbitrarily deprived of families; and so forth. Nevertheless, clinical practice and other forms of case services—the customary conditions of child welfare services—are particularly amenable to standard treatment controls and even placebo controls, particularly since standard practice has not been credibly validated. Yet, to the extent to which RCTs are not fully implemented for whatever reason, the resulting information is necessarily uncertain.

The human services have conducted a variety of prospective social experiments in support of specific social policies; many of these tests incorporated randomized designs. However, studies based on panel surveys such as the Panel Study of Income Dynamics (PSID), the National Longitudinal Study of Youth (NLSY), and the Survey of Income and Program Participation (SIPP) may be valuable as pilot investigations and even as preliminary assessments of interventions, but they cannot stand as decisive tests because of the debilitating problems of self-selection; there is no random assignment to control conditions in panel studies.

The sanction of a rational social experiment is particularly powerful since it provides a decisive test of the ability of an intervention to achieve its social objectives. However, the political influence of the experiments in public child welfare and in social services generally, especially because they routinely defy the canons of scientific procedures, depend on the degree to which they *appear* to be scientific and the degree to which political actors are willing to acknowledge their credibility. The experiments still exert a political influence in the absence of truly rational procedures.

The issue of method and proof is not a critic's quibble since both the child welfare literature and the broader scholarship of the social services have failed to even approximate randomized controls. Their nonrandomized controls (the quasi experiments) are porous; their before-and-after comparisons are inadequate. The research also suffers from many other invalidating weaknesses: limited data, unreliable measures, and a multitude of apparent researcher biases. Most studies are not national but rely on locally drawn convenience samples even when random assignment is a feature of the methodology. The literature's growing reliance on administrative data lacks tests of accuracy in spite of strong suspicions that caseworkers frequently write descriptions and diagnoses of children that they feel will achieve particular placement outcomes or justify services.[2] However, the utility of administrative records is undercut from the start by their long recognized unreliability and inaccuracy (Bush 1984). For example, in support of Bush's later observations that the tacit motives of agencies and workers corrupt case records, Sherman, Neuman, and Shyne (1973) document

> a general reluctance among child welfare workers to attribute the main or precipitating source of a problem to the child. An example of this was a case in the sample in which the worker described the problem . . . as follows: "Child caused physical damage to a younger sibling; playing with matches and threatening to burn the house and destroy his mother." Yet, those workers clicked off "Parent/child conflict". . . rather than "Child's emotional problem" as the main reason for placement. It is likely that the same terms and descriptions are used with great variability by different caseworkers.

But most problematic, hardly any study actually measures the child's outcomes and among those few that do, none employ reliable measures or reliable procedures.

The problems with research do not simply reflect the faults of the researchers; they clearly express society's lack of concern for the safety, health, and socialization of dependent children. It is astonishing that no systematic information system has ever existed to describe the public child welfare system while there is still no assurance that any comprehensive system will be implemented in the public sector (Committee on Ways and Means 1996:759–62). Indeed, it is quite likely that the continued preference to devolve service responsibility to the states will undermine recent efforts.

America's faith in science and technology, by confounding rational decision making with political decision making, has subverted the independence of the social sciences. The human services are part of the broader discipline of social science that informs the policy-making process. Social investigators may try to comply with the canons of scientific rationality for epistemological reasons, but organizationally they are frequently com-

---

2. The growing enthusiasm for administrative data (Barth et al. 1994; O'Brien, McClellan, and Alf 1992; Tatara 1993) is understandable in light of the appalling quality of information about the child welfare system.

pelled to conform with regnant expectations for their own roles in the drama of social competition. The primping for power and prestige does not entail scientific information; it does need to conform with social preferences. The rational ideal in social decision making is parodied more than pursued. The culture loves its scientists but only as far as its own traditions and intuitive, indeed surreal, social authority are maintained.

As a consequence of methodologically porous research and factional pressures to create obliging research findings, the outcomes of child welfare programs are at least indeterminate. Yet these programs are probably ineffective and may even be harmful when measured against any standard except the abuse visited on children by irresponsible parents. Without credibly testing its theories, the scholarship of child welfare is fated to senescence, chasing intellectual vitality with the wigs, implants, and facelifts of its experiments with truth.

A neglectful public has refused to approve the necessary funds for more credible research methods to investigate child welfare services. Moreover, the foster care system would be unlikely to tolerate objective scrutiny; few researchers or practitioners within the system are in positions to apply these designs dispassionately. The failure to successfully adapt science to child welfare practice—the quixotic notion of the social worker as researcher—has reduced all of the claims of the child welfare community to political statements that carry only the cachet of power, cultural convenience, and social compatibility. Without rational evidence for any production function except surveillance, child welfare services serve in ceremonial roles as symbols of popular values.

In spite of the conclusion that no conclusion is possible and notwithstanding perhaps a century of research efforts—indeed, child welfare may be the oldest subspecialty of American social welfare scholarship—there is still little if any accurate information, either descriptive or evaluative, about child welfare services. The system appears to be avoiding scrutiny and this in itself is cause to question the quality and social role of current provisions for maltreated children. Plausible suspicion about the child welfare system, especially in light of its gruesome history (Bremner 1970–71; Kadushin 1974), places the burden of proof not with the skeptic but on the shoulders of those responsible for care and those who have freely taken on the task of evaluating that care.

Chapter 1 presents two case studies of children in congregate foster care. The children are both in their middle teens; both have spent many years in the system and in a variety of placements; and both have finally reached Boys Town, Nevada, a residential treatment setting where they will most likely remain until they age out of care. Although largely based on the experiences of two children, the case histories are composites, leaving out some actual experiences and adding others. The changes ensure anonymity for the children while illustrating the problems of the public system, conveying a portrait more telling than any few children can offer.

The case studies are not intended to provide analytic authority for any conclusion. That is the task of chapters 2 and 3. Rather, the case studies are presented to ground perceptions in the specifics of care and to provide reference points for the succeeding discussions.

Information concerning Natalie and Adam was obtained from state records as well as from sustained and intensive interviews with the children over more than half a year. Interviews were also conducted with their relatives, schoolteachers and counselors, caseworkers, therapists, physicians, police, foster parents, group home workers, cottage parents, friends, and others. In short, attempts were made to interview anyone who knew the children.

A problem of representativeness naturally remains. The literature is too weak to provide any authoritative description of the typical child. Of course, some children, although probably very few, come out of care and go on to become stellar citizens. However, to justify the system on the basis of these very few is to ignore its failures for the many. There is a strong suspicion, fueled by an enormous number of known failures and tragedies of children in care, that the system harms many of its charges to an indictable extent. The fact remains that little effort has been made to audit the quality and outcomes of the child welfare system in spite of routine observations of the compelling problems of many of its charges and the common deficiencies of placements, caregivers, and workers.

Chapter 2 characterizes the problems and political functions of the public child welfare system—its ideological dimensions—and then goes on to analyze the descriptive studies of care—its dynamics (e.g., lengths of stay and dispositions), utilization, and quality. Chapter 3 elaborates on the experimental tests of service effectiveness. Both chapters argue that public child welfare services routinely fail to provide care at common levels of American decency and to effectively address the personal problems of children. The level at which care is provided, the conditions of the children, and the results of their years in care undercut the society's claims to compassion. The many published evaluations of care are invariably incomplete and poorly conducted. The experiments either to improve existing care or to provide better alternatives have failed as scientifically credible research. They have also failed to substantiate the effectiveness of any program intervention. In the end, the child welfare literature has been molded by the professional ambitions of its authors and the political imperatives of a parsimonious society rather than by the realities of children.

The absence of good information is itself part of the problem, exacerbated by the active ambitions of the field's researchers. Child welfare research had been chafing under even its light bridle of methodology, so it simply took it off. As the unfortunate result, the authority of the field's claims cannot transcend the postmodern oddity of "memoirist-reportage" (Oates 1998).[3]

Still, the research has by and large achieved at least a minimal honesty that permits reanalysis of its methods and conclusions largely on the basis of published data. Nevertheless, the limitations of the research appear to stem from more than the limitations of data and funding. The literature consistently reflects a particular point of view that corresponds with contemporary social preferences. It is therefore inadvisable, and even irresponsible, to ignore its ideological dimensions and political congruence.

The poor quality of the research and its political tropism indict the competence and independence of its community of researchers—largely academic social workers and social scientists. Since a "community of the competent" justifies both academic standing and academic freedom (Haskell 1996), the children in public care might be better served by shifting the responsibility for evaluating public child welfare services to more developed disciplines. Indeed, the research record of modern society's semiprofessions generally argues for a return to the core academic disciplines, even though they have frequently been betrayed by the social scientists themselves.

The analysis and reinterpretation of the child welfare literature lead in chapter 4, the conclusion, to a political explanation—the popularity of the doctrine of social efficiency—for what the children may need but are not receiving in order to mature into valuable citizens. Shortcuts to socialization, notably including the range of contemporary social welfare strategies for dependent children and families at risk of dissolution, are probably impossible; parsimonious interventions have certainly failed to demonstrate their effectiveness. Rather, more intensive surrogate care for many more children is probably necessary to replicate critical experiences that they

---

3. Indeed, with its disregard for the canons of science, child welfare research and social service research in general are becoming vulnerable to competition from the humanities. As one example, Oates's (1998) "memoirist-reportage" looks like rudimentary social science; however, the referents for its authority lie in the reporter and not in any claim for an objective reality. "Memoirist-reportage is a genre with an obvious appeal for contemporary tastes in which the 'personal' (including the frankly confessional) is freely mixed with the 'impersonal'" (Oates 1998:12). Unfortunately, most of the child welfare literature is little better than the researchers' memoirs. Yet hypocritically, the social science research adopts a form of investigation and report that implicitly invokes the credibility of science even while lacking its substance.

missed in their own families. However, American society is not willing to bear the expense of adequate surrogate care, addicted as it is to a faith in social efficiency.

Both neglect and parsimony mock the needs of children in public care, and therefore a strategy of generosity is all that is left. Generosity of the heart needs to be expressed as generosity of the purse. Much greater public spending on children and families is required to repair social problems in the United States. However, this spending is unlikely, creating a true dilemma of social policy that liberals have unfortunately abided with a self-defeating equanimity.

Social acceptance of any public policy typically occurs without the rational validation of its likely effects and largely for reasons of political advantage: compatibility, personal authority, advantage, or professional standing. In this way, acceptance may have little to do with the actual production function of social services—their ability to remedy social problems. The tatters of existing research cannot be stitched together into credible estimates of the reality of care. Rather, without a true ability to address their defining social problems, services may serve as symbols—ceremonies in the play of power. Indeed, this is probably the true role of the child welfare system with its so-called scientific research serving as an apologist for social denial and the child welfare worker acting as a compliant extension of her culture.

Las Vegas with its gated communities and attenuated public spirit is a stark expression of national political preferences, stripped of any softening rhetoric. In Las Vegas, civic virtue drowns in the bath of the casino owners' self-love and greed. The public adores them. Yet, for all their pampered fastidiousness and cunningly manufactured image of philanthropy and good will, the casino owners control the odds and the miserly budgets of the Nevada legislature. Nevada, the seventh wealthiest state in the nation, cheaps out on public education, higher education, public parks and recreation, and child welfare services.

Nevada is an arid reminder that the wealthiest nation in the history of the world—wealthier than it has ever been—refuses to address the needs of its most blameless citizens. In a similar way and with only rare exceptions during its history, the United States seems willing to embrace almost any excuse to reduce public responsibility.

Children Who Could Have Been

1
Natalie and Adam

Natalie

Natalie just turned eighteen. Her father had begun fondling her when she was seven and raped her when she was twelve. At the time that she was raped, Natalie was living at home under the supervision of the child welfare system.

When she was seven, her father had insisted on applying topical medication to her vagina for a yeast infection. He called her into the bathroom and had her strip and lie on her back with her legs spread in the air while he applied the ointment. Fifteen minutes passed. Her mother was cooking in the kitchen.

Shortly afterward, he began visiting her bedroom waiting until he thought she was asleep. He took off her pajama bottoms and panties, spread her legs apart slowly so as not to awaken her, and rubbed his hands over her undeveloped breasts and vagina. Occasionally he would penetrate her lightly with his finger or open his pants and rub himself on her. Next he went to the bathroom and then back to bed.

He worked nights and her mother worked during the day. Natalie came home from school in the afternoons to her father, who played games with her that allowed him to touch her body under her clothes. He insisted that she not tell anyone; these were secret games between daddy and Natalie.

The touching and fondling scared her as her father groomed her for his pleasure. She faked sleeping, lying rigidly with her eyes pressed closed while her father roamed her body with his hands. Eventually she told her mother. When her mother spoke to her father, he denied fondling Natalie but acknowledged that he helped her apply the ointment. Her father beat her with a belt the next day for going to her mother. Her mother instructed her not to sleep without clothes. Natalie began to wet her bed almost daily.

Her father beat her often and the beatings usually involved fondling. He beat her for complaining, for lying, for avoiding her homework, for being messy. At times, he had her strip off her panties and lie across his lap. He often removed her tops. Sometimes her mother was at home; sometimes she was at work. Sometimes she sent her daughter to her husband for discipline, asking God for protection.

A couple, friends of her parents, stayed over for a few days on a visit. The husband found Natalie alone in the garage one day and ran his hands over her body, telling her what a lovely girl she was and how much he liked her. Frightened and hurt, she complained to her mother, who became angry, insisting that Natalie was lying again.

A few days before her twelfth birthday, she told a schoolteacher that her father frequently touched her under her clothes. The teacher had her speak with the school counselor, who called the police. Natalie was removed from her home and placed in a temporary shelter for children. A hearing was held in juvenile court two weeks later. Her father was ordered to leave the home and enter counseling. He was allowed visits but only when his wife was present. After two weeks in the shelter, Natalie was returned to her home. Her father had moved out but he came by two or three times each week for dinner and to see his wife.

After about three months of visiting, her father moved back into the house. The court suspended supervision a few months later. Her father never admitted to the counselor that he fondled her. The touching was just inadvertent roughhousing and the application of the ointment was bad judgment. Counseling was terminated after a few sessions because the therapist felt that nothing was to be gained without a confession.

One Sunday, shortly after her father moved back into the house and while her mother was downstairs cleaning, Natalie went into her parents' bedroom to wake up her father for church. She got on the bed. He pulled down her pajamas, pinned her arms, rolled on top of her. She felt a sharp pain. When he was done, he told her not to tell anyone. She went into the bathroom to clean semen and blood off of her vagina and belly.

The rapes continued a few times each week over the next months. Her father had intercourse with Natalie at home after school and sometimes after she had gone to bed. He raped her on two outings to the lake while her mother was some distance away on the shore. Her father played shark. Natalie would dive under the water to retrieve colored pebbles. Her father would swim up to her and pull her under. He took off her swimming bottoms and penetrated her. She cleaned herself in the water.

Her father worked intermittently as a salad preparer, busboy, and porter in hotels. Her mother was a chambermaid. Married for more than twenty years, they moved to Las Vegas for work. The parents earned enough to get by; the little they saved carried them through times when her father was out of work. They were able to pay off a mortgage on a small house. The additional rent that her father had to pay when the court removed him from the house was a burden on their finances, eliminating Natalie's few frugal rewards—movies, pizza, toys.

Seven years younger than his wife, Natalie's father was a natty man with a thin moustache. Natalie's mother was more than forty years older than her and had aged noticeably, being very wrinkled and a bit stooped. People frequently asked if she was Natalie's grandmother and her father's mother. Her mother insists that Natalie is her natural child. However, Natalie's first caseworker discovered that the West Coast hospital named on Natalie's birth certificate had no record of admitting her mother.

Natalie frequently asks if she was adopted. She wants to own a history and to set both her parents and the rapes in perspective. Her mother stolidly denies that she was adopted even though it is becoming apparent that she is lying.

Natalie's mother is a superstitiously observant Catholic who believes that God is responsible for the good in her life and that the Devil is responsible for the bad. She is responsible for nothing, including sacrificing her daughter to keep her husband. Each room in her house contains a crucifix, and representations of Christ are on the walls. She appears lively and pleasant, pinching the cheeks of her caseworkers and Natalie's caretakers and making sure that there is some small gift in her shopping bags for everyone during her visits to Natalie. She is also secretive and untrusting, burying her own acquiescence with her husband's predatory sexuality under religious obedience. According to one of the therapists who saw her, "She always saw problems as either black or white and they were usually intractable and beyond her ability to control."

Over the years, she has freighted Natalie with the guilt of her love while criticizing her at every opportunity for anger, tight clothes, heavy cosmetics, disobedience, poor school grades, disrespect, seductiveness, and beauty. She rummages through Natalie's existence, searching for faults that might excuse her own inattention to Natalie's welfare. On her part, Natalie pleads for honesty from her mother. As she writes in one of her poems:

> All I have ever cared about, all I have
> ever had, I'm slowly losing day by day
>
> All I want is to hear an "I'm sorry" or
> "Yes, I was wrong."

During her mother's five years of meetings with counselors, therapists, cottage parents, and caseworkers, "I'm sorry" has been the last thing she is willing to say. To the contrary, she lists for Natalie's therapists the faults that she wants them to correct, as if she were sending a car that was still under warranty to a mechanic for a tune-up.

When Natalie was almost sixteen, her mother took her to a shopping mall for lunch. Natalie became caustic and accusatory, "You never care for me." Her mother spat back, "You deserve what your father did to you." Indeed, her mother is on a religious journey for absolution in denial of Natalie's search for understanding and acceptance.

Natalie was a lively child but as the rapes continued she became increasingly quiet and withdrawn. A counselor at a winter program at the local Y inquired about her changed mood. Natalie told her that her father was raping her. The physical examinations supported her claim that she was having sexual intercourse; her drawings for a therapist were explicit. The medical examinations also disclosed that she had pelvic inflammatory disease consequent to gonorrhea. She was removed from the house and again placed in the temporary shelter. She was thirteen.

Natalie began therapy withdrawn to the point of muteness. Her therapist asked Natalie to write down her feelings toward her father:

> Hey, you fucking bastard prick. You are a motherfuckin stupid ass bitch. If I ever see your motherfuckin ass on the fuckin streets I swear on the Holy Bible I will beat the fuckin hell of shit out of you and I guarantee I will cut your fuckin ass dick off and shove it down your motherfuckin throat. I don't ever want to see your fuckin ass ever again in my fuckin life you fuckin cunt. I don't know why the fuck you did this to me but deep down I'm hurt inside, depressed and ashamed that my own Biological Fuckin Father raped me and I will always hate you for the rest of my life, even though you don't want me to, you fuckin cunt. I don't know what the hell you think I am to you, but I'm not your fuckin sex toy. And if you were that desperate for sex you could have done it with my fuckin ass mom who neglected me when I told her about it or any other fuckin bitch that probably wouldn't have wanted it either or would have gotten sick because of your fuckin sicknesses which have put me in more problems and dangers. That's all I have to fuckin say to you, you fuckin bastard.

Natalie also loathes her mother for abandoning her to her father's depravity, indeed, for choosing the small security of her husband's occasional paychecks and a marriage, however unsatisfying, over her daughter's safety and emotional security. Natalie identifies powerfully with teenage heroines whose deepest fears have been realized by parents who abandon them.

> Her hatred for her mother wasn't rational, but it was so passionately felt that it took the place of the pain she would not allow herself to feel. Hate flooded through her, filled her with so much demonic energy that she was nearly able to toss the heavy beam off her legs.
>
> *Damn you to Hell, Mama.*

The top floor of the house caved in upon the ground floor with a sound like cannons blasting.

Damn you, Mama! Damn you!

The first two floors of flaming rubble broke through the already weakened cellar ceiling.

Mama — (Koontz 1981:13)

Even though Natalie says that she understands the harm that her parents have done to her, she still feels beyond all reason that she is to blame. She cannot shed the anxiety that she deserves her mother's hostility: Natalie feels that in some still undiscovered way she is an unforgivably flawed daughter.

She rages at the unfairness of it all, burdened with the perpetual, inescapable noise of her undeserved guilt. She is marked by her mother's harsh judgments and her constant search for evidence of Natalie's guilt — signs that she seduced her father. Natalie rebels by defiance but harms herself further. The trap closes tighter as her rebellions appear to confirm her mother's judgments, further swelling Natalie's anger and hopelessness.

Natalie stayed in the shelter for a few weeks. Her new caseworker, after reviewing the case file and chatting with her for an hour, placed her with a foster mother, Millie, who provided care in her home for three other foster children along with her own two daughters, one sixteen and the other, Suzie, a nineteen year old with a baby but no husband. Millie also had a married twenty-six-year-old daughter who had two children. The caseworker hoped that Natalie would fit in since the only other choice was a more confining placement in a group foster home.

Millie's husband, a hotel porter who drank too much, had left her some years before with small children. Millie worked part time as a cashier; the foster care payments — about four hundred dollars per month for each child — put a thin cushion under the family. Millie did not adequately control her own children and was no match for Natalie's "demonic energy." Natalie came to Millie's home as a withdrawn and fearful child. She learned from her new foster brothers and sisters to express her anger at the world, ignoring punishments and restrictions.

She thought that Millie's daughter Suzie was terrific and tried to copy her clothes, makeup, and toughness. In spite of her baby, Suzie had a number of avid suitors and was in no rush to marry; she dressed provocatively, smoked, experimented with drugs, and proved her independence with a quick temper. Everyone in the home, except Millie, had a fast temper and was quick to take offense.

Natalie tried to become Suzie and by thirteen and one-half years old was regularly dating older teenagers and men, one in his thirties. Over the past year Natalie had matured from a bony child into a beautiful and shapely young woman with generous breasts and sexually inviting manners. She dramatized her eyes with thick bands of mascara that were carried toward her temples in "Egyptian girl" style; her lips were glossy and thick with a heavy layer of lipstick. She pouted and posed, dressing in tiny skirts, the tightest and smallest of shorts, and low-cut, see-through blouses. Natalie had been taught that there were no sexual boundaries.

She began to smack the other children when they displeased her. She had virtually stopped caring for herself as though to wear dirtiness as a badge of guilt, a symbol of her personal degradation. Instead of washing herself and her clothes, she masked her odors under heavy floral scents. Her grades at school were poor. She continued to wet her bed. After nine months, Millie and the caseworker agreed that Natalie needed a setting in which she could be better disciplined, especially to control her growing and indiscriminate belligerence toward adults. One morning, her caseworker showed up to announce that she would be moved that afternoon. Natalie said goodbye to Millie and two of the girls who were there for lunch.

Natalie was moved to Camilla Park Home, a group program that cared for twenty-five teenage girls. The caseworker's plan also provided for ongoing psychotherapy to handle her behavioral problems as well as a referral to a urologist for the bedwetting.

Camilla Park is a nonprofit, church-run agency. In contrast to the four hundred dollars per month that Millie was paid to care for Melissa, the state paid Camilla Park seventy-six dollars for each day of care—about twenty-eight thousand dollars annually. From the outside, Camilla Park looks like a very large private home. It is located in an older, small-home suburb of Las Vegas. The neighbors do not attend to children who are not theirs.

Camilla Park is shabby and unclean, publicizing its inattention to the needs of the resident children. The large living room is furnished with warped and chipped furniture; its carpet is stained, dusty, and worn; its walls need plaster and paint. The blinds and windows are dirty. The Heidi reproductions on the wall, a mockery of pastoral tranquility and the sanctity of childhood, look like exiles from a hospital pediatric ward. The girls' bedrooms lead off a long, dingy corridor. Three girls sleep in each small room, also seemingly furnished from the local Salvation Army Thrift Shop. The rooms are cluttered with dirty clothing, cosmetics, tattered school-books, and paper. Beds are not made. The kitchen counters are encrusted; the refrigerator is dirty and cluttered; the stove is greasy. There are signs of roaches. The locked, glass-enclosed staff office stands over the home like a guard tower.

Girls do their homework at the congregate dining room table or in the living room, sitting on the frayed sofas and writing on their laps. A radio is always blaring music somewhere in the home, adding to the din of the television. The few staff talk among themselves.

Camilla Park is understaffed. Its personnel are inadequately prepared to care for the residents. A maximum of nine staff members—and usually fewer as turnover is high—have twenty-four-hour, near total responsibility for about twenty-five troubled girls. Camilla Park management seeks out the least expensive and docile employees, hoping they are able to control the children. Yet the staff, ignorant of any method to control the girls' anger, routinely fail to win their respect.

During the day, there are frequently too few staff to take the girls to their appointments and still cover the home; as a result, many scheduled meetings with physicians and therapists are aborted; many recreational outings are missed. There has never been sufficient staff to adequately supervise activities in the home and to offer the girls extended time to discuss themselves. Staff rarely help the girls with their schoolwork or demonstrate any interest in their education. Few of the staff act as mentors or reasonable substitute parents. Most never develop special relationships with the residents.

In 1996, Camilla Park paid its manager nine dollars per hour. She received no benefits until she had worked there for six months and then only health coverage. Until she entered a formal complaint to the state wage board, Camilla Park refused to pay her for the overtime she put in, claiming that she was a professional, salaried employee. Yet she had still not graduated from college and had only one and one-half years of relevant previous experience.

None of the other staff at Camilla Park had graduated from college; only two others were enrolled in any college program; many of the staff had not graduated from high school, although they had earned graduate equivalency degrees. They picked up information about children and their needs haphazardly from their contacts with psychologists, social workers, and more experienced staff in other agencies (usually the state's Department of Child and Family Services). Camilla Park refused to invest in specialized training courses, seminars, consultations, or formal staff development programs. So long as the children were usually controlled, administrators at the church charity that ran Camilla Park were content.

The church organization that runs Camilla Park is one of the larger sectarian charity organizations typical of the Catholic, Episcopalian, Jewish, Lutheran, Mormon, Baptist, Methodist, and other sectarian charities. It also manages child and family service agencies, recreational and athletic clubs for youth, cultural organizations, mental health programs, shelters for the homeless, counseling programs, programs for the physically and mentally debilitated, and an annual campaign for funds. The state's per diem rate includes the charity's costs for supervising Camilla Park and thereby subsidizes the charity organization's broader activities, including its prominence in the community, and its general leadership of the community's social services.

The Camilla Park staff had many of the same emotional and social problems as the children they were supposed to heal. One counselor was a methamphetamine addict. Another stole from the residents. A third had severe emotional impairments and stormed at the youths as they blazed at her. A male counselor was having a sexual liaison with an underage teenager who lived nearby. Their couplings took place at Camilla Park; he posted one of the girls as a lookout.

The staff routinely humiliated the girls as a disciplinary device. There was little respect for their privacy, and male staff freely intruded into their bedrooms. Staff were authoritarian, rigid, and cold, occasionally employing corporal punishment. The few hardworking, warm employees left within a year or became hardened themselves.

Natalie was dropped into the oppositional, violent, and belligerent youth subculture of foster care among teenage girls who were as angry as she. Many had gone through greater abuse. One of her roommates, at ten years old, had been prostituted by her father at a construction site where he worked; he had been raping her for the previous three years. Others were routinely beaten by parents who were drug addicts, emotionally disturbed, mentally impaired, or simply evil. Many of their parents were socially incompetent, having few skills, little motivation, and even less concern for their children. Camilla Park tolerated, and even encouraged, the tough and vicious survival ethos of their residents. The girls prized their ability to block emotions, to take abuse and pain without complaining, and to defy any authority. They humiliated, beat, and abused each other.

For a long while, the girls at Camilla Park had been conducting pajama night initiations. They would camp out with the new girl in the living room. When she finally fell asleep the others would pounce on her and "beat her to crap." This was finally stopped but a new girl went through months of taunting, intimidation, and abuse until the veteran residents were convinced that she "could take it and survive." On occasion, the staff gleefully participated in the hazing. Those who could not survive were placed at other programs.

Like similar group homes, Camilla Park has a nominal system of rewards and punishments, frequently based on some vague enthusiasm for behavioral therapy: obedience to rules is rewarded, disobedience is punished with "consequences," usually the deprivation of privileges such as watching television, freedom of the grounds, and permission to leave the campus. Punishments and rewards are applied mechanically with little emotion except derision when a staff member feels buoyed by a child's discomfort. "The fucking rules" infrequently address the individual circumstances of the children.

Still, most of the girls go their own way. Aside from being back for curfew and attending school regularly, they are largely free to spend their time as they wish. Most of the girls are sexually active, engaging in athletic, dispassionate couplings with a series of men and boys. They are expert at separating sex from feeling. Few are doing well at school; many are regularly truant in spite of Camilla Park's house rules. The girls largely interact with each other and their friends without the supervision of staff.

The girls smoke pot; some use speed, "shrooms," and acid. Almost all drink and smoke. They are supplied by their boyfriends, relatives, and occasionally by staff. For lack of inexpensive alternatives, the state continues to license programs like Camilla Park in which staff and foster parents run their homes like gang clubhouses.

Natalie was spared the pajama party but because of her beauty and charm, she went through an unusually tough initiation at Camilla Park. The girls taunted her without mercy for being dirty and wetting her bed. One of the staff, jealous of her, frequently started belittling attacks. The girls stigmatized Natalie as a "whore" and humiliated her for attracting men. At other times, they ignored and isolated her.

Natalie became even more sexually provocative, constantly teasing and flirting with all men. She bragged among the girls of her prowess, cunning, coldness, and power to seduce. She went out to prove it. The girls retaliated. The staff did not interfere.

In spite of her outward show, Natalie was probably not sexually active at Camilla Park; she acted out an assigned whorish role as part of the youth drama of the group home. She was actually frightened of both sex and men. The prospect of sex did not recall her power over men but rather her loss of control over her body and her hopeless entrapment by predatory adults. Sex forced an intimacy that terrified her.

Natalie was customarily passive in adapting both to the harsh subculture of youth and to the adult world. Putting up only a short act of defiance, she accepted the leadership of the other girls, as she appeared to smilingly defer to adults, at least initially. She bragged and occasionally threw a tantrum when control became intolerable and she needed to create room for herself. But she had learned from teachers, therapists, counselors, and notably her parents, to reinforce their expectations of her. She had been groomed for obedience but not for the truth.

Natalie's schoolwork continued to decline. Occasionally she cut classes. She ran away for a day from Camilla Park on two occasions. Her plans to flee to another state with a friend were "ratted out" by the friend's sister. She wanted to "screw around—going to dances, being with friends." She was disruptive in school and frequently disciplined.

She spent an increasing amount of time relaxing with popular fiction and writing poetry and stories, displaying a talent for words and ideas. The school, however, misconstrued her personal problems and rebellious- ness as signs of intellectual limitation, defining her mediocre performance and her choice of vocational courses as the best that could be expected of her. Natalie further disengaged from an undemanding but regimented schooling.

The girls eventually accepted her. Indeed, one of their leaders became her close friend. Jackie was a very large, heavy young woman with a mis- chievous intelligence—she rewired the alarm system to be able to bypass it whenever she chose—who took pleasure from physical violence. Natalie became close with a counselor, a young woman who won the regard of the other girls and who made herself accessible to them. She particularly enjoyed spending time with Natalie. Natalie also developed a close rela- tion with Cynthia, her new caseworker, an attractive young mother whom Natalie began to emulate.

Yet, in spite of adapting to her peers, developing a supportive rela- tionship with a staff member, and finding an attentive caseworker, Camilla Park did not work out for Natalie. The staff member who had taken an in- tense dislike to Natalie made her life there unbearable. She stole from the girls, snorted speed when she was on duty, and displayed an explosive tem- per to the girls and even to coworkers. Her mother worked in the central administration of the charity. Natalie was given five hours notice that she was being moved to one of the Leisse Homes. The worker stayed on.

> Bounced around from place to place,
>   I am nothing but a part of generation "throw-away"
> I've no good friends, I have no life;
>   My mother still thinks that I have lied.
>
>   Natalie

The Leisse Homes, a profit-making agency one step down the ladder of comfort and care from Camilla Park, operated in four locations, each providing care for eight residents. Infused with a romantic distortion of an earlier and equally callous period in American life, President Ronald Reagan and the conservative revival had imposed profit and privatization on social services as the panacea for failed public care. With the epiphany of the entrepreneur, Leisse Homes was created to profit financially from youth care.

In fact, it succeeded famously to demonstrate the effect of business on human services. The director and owner, a social worker with a newly minted graduate degree who put even less effort into her studies than her residents, drove a seventy thousand-dollar Jaguar within three years of serving the first child. The children at the Leisse Homes, however, did not fare as well, living out Oliver Twist's more unpleasant experiences.

Leisse Homes also received a per diem of seventy-six dollars and while it budgeted for multiple staff, it usually provided only a single staff person for each of its locations, even during the afternoon and evening when the girls' needs for companionship, transportation, and supervision were the greatest. The staff received less training and were more poorly paid than those at Camilla Park. Ms. Leisse, who was a licensed clinical social worker by the time that Natalie arrived, provided the sole supervision for all of the staff at the four locations.

Ms. Leisse was a friendly, motherly woman about forty-five years old who had a knack for ingratiating herself. She acknowledged a multitude of problems with her homes, promising to quickly correct them. She was deeply sincere in expressing gratitude to those who brought problems to her attention personally; this, after all, she explained, is the way that broken dishes get replaced. It is impossible to dislike Ms. Leisse; it is also impossible to trust her.

Things do not change and the state's surveillance and licensing process is hampered by the lack of alternative placements. The food is dull and repetitious, a monotony of reconstituted mashed potatoes, bread, canned vegetables, ham, and fried chicken. The homes are rarely staffed up to budgeted levels. Incompetent staff are not fired—everyone, Ms. Leisse explains, deserves another chance. The staff are rarely supervised and the overriding, near exclusive concern is to maintain order. Many of the girls, particularly in two of the homes, are also heavily sedated, and many are obese. Ms. Leisse has translated neglect into training for independence, encouraging the girls to care for themselves but providing little adult guidance and even less attention to their emotional states, schooling, clothing, personal hygiene, and medical and dental care. The girls routinely miss appointments; there is no follow-up with teachers and counselors; they frequently are truant; many run away. Not surprisingly, many of the girls, including Natalie, who was placed among the best functioning girls, deteriorated at the Leisse Homes.

Ms. Leisse obligingly offered to provide care for the most troubled youths, and the state, desperately short of funds and foster homes, always hoped that somehow and against all experience, a child who was difficult to place might still find some comfort in Ms. Leisse's chubby embrace. But the Leisse Homes provided only an environment of formal behavioral rules that were arbitrarily enforced.

Natalie certainly did not find any asylum at the Leisse Homes. Her relations with boys, largely unsupervised, became even more seductive. Her relations with the girls in the home were frequently violent. Her new high school put her in special education classes even though she tested among the brightest in verbal ability and reading achievement. She frequently missed appointments with her therapist.

Her visits with her mother were also unsupervised. Those meetings became increasingly painful as her mother probed for evidence of Natalie's blame, pressing the theme of Natalie's complicity in her father's depravity. Natalie's sexual provocativeness while at Camilla Park and the Leisse Homes disturbed her mother's sense of propriety but also showed the world that if her husband did do anything it was Natalie's fault, not the result of her own failure as a mother. Indeed, her mother bought the alluring clothes and the cosmetics that Natalie demanded. Natalie thought that she was gaining a victory of control over her mother, but her mother was dressing her in guilt.

The other girls in the home, intensely jealous of her allure, picked up on Natalie's self-doubts and put her through a scalding initiation. They accused her of seducing her father and continued the theme of her being promiscuous and shameless. At times she was isolated and ostracized; no one would speak to her; they glared at her and rolled their eyes. They wrote "slut" on her towels and her dressing mirror. They chanted whore, whore, whore, whenever she tried to say anything. They pointed and whispered behind their hands.

> It's really hard living
>   in this world
> Where everyone thinks you're
>   a whore.
>
> But what they don't know
>   is that the little
>   whore
> Is the girl next door.
>   Natalie

They were also vile to each other in an endless round of cruelty. A fifteen year old had obsessive thoughts about killing and death. One of her two roommates spoke into her sleeping ear, "The skeletons of the people you want to kill are knocking on the windows." The other roommate knocked on the wall. The whole house awoke to her screams and the roommates' laughter. Some of the girls at the Leisse Home became psychotic.

Ms. Leisse solved the staffing problem at Natalie's home by hiring a childless, live-in couple. Vigo and Astrida were two physicians trained in Lithuania who were in their fifties. They had emigrated to the United States in 1992 after the Soviet bloc had cracked but were not able to pass the licensing exam in any state. They believed in homeopathic medicine, mind cures, and a variety of alternative medical treatments, including acupuncture, massage, and meditation. Their English was barely intelligible and they squabbled among themselves constantly in Lithuanian. Vigo enjoyed barging into the girls' rooms in the morning when they were dressing. He checked on them when their showers lasted too long. They were paid as a couple at the rate of $17,500 per year and given health benefits.

Astrida began accusing Natalie of trying to seduce Vigo. Vigo at the same time was beginning to eye Natalie. Both of them took every opportunity to criticize, taunt, and bedevil her; they egged on the other girls. Natalie toughed it out, making friends at school, singing in a choral group, writing poetry, and reading. After seven months, the caseworker, Cynthia, who had been following Natalie closely, finally succeeded in placing her at Boys Town.

Natalie was fifteen when she came to Boys Town. Her hygiene had improved and her bed wetting was less frequent but she was seriously behind in high school, which had tracked her as a "special needs" student with little potential for college. The counselors at school treated her as an object of charity needing pity and protection. None of them picked up on her skills enough to inquire into her academic performance.

Natalie had suppressed her temper but only in service to a highly manipulative approach to adults and social situations. Natalie was an accomplished and fluent liar for reasons of convenience and of psychological comfort. The lies allowed her to ignore behaviors that contradicted her protective beliefs and to hide her vulnerabilities. There was no one at the time she left the Leisse Home that she would confide in. Even her relationship with Cynthia was compartmentalized and guarded by a very careful presentation of herself, denying any threat to her persona of cooperation, admiration, affability, charm, and obedience.

When she first came to Boys Town, she was receiving a constant stream of calls from boys and men. She was outwardly sexual and even began claiming that she was bisexual, bragging that she liked sex with girls. Her roommate confronted her one day, "Why are you lying like this?" Natalie answered, "Because I am that way. I lie."

Her cottage parents at Boys Town insisted that she discourage the constant calls, that she become less seductive with men, that she dress more modestly, that she attend to her schoolwork, and that she conform to the house rules. Her cottage parents also tried to convince Natalie that she had more to offer than a body. She appeared relieved that limits were being set.

At eighteen years old, she uses little makeup. Her clothes are not overtly provocative. Since arriving at Boys Town she has had only a few relations with young men, and they have been just a bit older than she. She insists that these relations have not involved intercourse and she hopes to be chaste until she marries. She has joined a church. Her participation in school has become more intense and her grades improved, at least for a while. She has friends at school and at her cottage. She is preparing to leave Boys Town. She expects to redo a number of courses in order to become eligible for college.

At times, she even appears to enjoy a sense of personal capacity, relaxing into her expectations of a reasonable future. Still, under stress, she retreats into fantasies of who she is and what she can do. Her behavior and her moods are still erratic.

Boys Town made its greatest contribution to Natalie by stopping the abuse of foster care itself. The cottage parents at Boys Town have their own children and it is apparent to the residents that they are not substitute parents. Yet the cottage parents are affectionate and supportive. They try to understand the needs of the children; they are always available to them and they reach out to the children. They are never abusive; they do not tolerate the predatory youth culture of penal institutions.

The Boys Town residents finally settle in. They and Boys Town accept the relative permanence of their placement; they will be there until they graduate from high school. Boys Town nearly doubles the state's subsidy with its own funds. The additional money purchases competent staff, appropriate supervision, and a secure and comforting physical environment. Unlike any of Natalie's previous placements, Boys Town provides the core experiences for youth: stability, the presence of caring, responsible, affectionate adults, controls on behavior, the supports for emotional security, a decent physical environment, the sense of being valued, an opportunity to learn self-discipline, and most important, the patience of time and money to allow the lessons of decency to take hold.

The state poses the greatest challenge to the Boys Town residents. It considers Boys Town to be a therapeutic placement, implying that after children are stabilized, they should be moved to less expensive levels of care, and preferably with a foster family. This catch–22 implies that those who improve are penalized by being separated from the only decent environment that many of them have known and the likely cause of their improvements. More perversely, those who remain by dint of having failed to adapt probably require a far more structured and intensive placement but get stalled at Boys Town. These children are trapped in the pretense of care at an intermediate level unless of course their behavior deteriorates to psychosis and they are transferred to psychiatric settings. In this perverse Peter Principle of foster care, children endure a level of care at least one step below what they need, washing back and forth in the surf between bare maintenance and active abuse.

The state workers and the Boys Town staff—all aware of the callousness of public policy and its obeisance to penury—bend reports in order to maintain the continuity of placements. Thus the operant but tacit incentives of the child care system frustrate accountability by inspiring official documents and reports that create fictions about the actual situations of the children in care. Naturally, research that draws on these records is necessarily inaccurate and misleading.

Yet Boys Town also makes unfortunate concessions, putting more effort into a seemingly futile effort to prepare their children for a glorified independence than to realize their abilities or expand their limitations. Boys Town's concessions take on mythic proportions in terms of teaching obedience, respect, and the work ethic: encouraging children to save for their emancipation while teaching them to fit into the work force. Natalie has worked at a variety of menial jobs, usually as a waitress and food preparer in fast food restaurants and usually for twenty hours each week. Yet talented children like Natalie are not introduced to an enriched culture: they rarely receive music, dance, or art lessons; they seldom attend concerts and plays; child care workers of one sort or another and psychotherapists are virtually the only middle-class professionals they encounter. Less gifted children are not exposed to the opportunities of the American culture or prepared for citizenship. There is some amount of popular fiction in Natalie's cottage; some of the girls have collected a small number of horror, romance, and mystery stories; and the cottage contains the obligatory encyclopedia. Yet Natalie is not led to literature or provided any exposure to a subculture of ideas. Working-class and poor kids have their destinies fixed by foster care, even the best of it.

Natalie may be one of the very few foster children who succeed, but as one of her workers remarked it will probably be a sad success after years of searching for a place in life. The Boys Town cottage parents cannot name more than a handful of children among the hundreds they have known who have gone on to productive lives. Natalie's future is clouded. She remains a troubled young woman constantly searching for a way to regenerate a relationship with her parents and obsessed with dispelling her deep feelings of guilt and anger.

She talks about going back to live with her parents . . . at least for a few weeks or months until she can get a stable job. She is in therapy once every few weeks negotiating a reconciliation with her mother and father. The reconciliation, however, is unlikely and probably not in her best interests since her father refuses to acknowledge the fondling and the rapes, let alone his conscious actions in grooming her for his use.

Her mother still sides with her husband, insisting that Natalie is a liar, enumerating the many instances in which she has lied, and picking over Natalie's many indiscretions and provocations. Her mother repeats at every opportunity how much she loves her, how much she cares, and how lonely she is without her. But each statement of affection is followed by the sighing hope that Natalie change her ways and become a dutiful child. Natalie says, see, I am changing. But her parents only see her deceptions and deviousness. Natalie has not learned to accept the fact of her parents' hostile depravity. They do not love her and she does not love herself.

A sage once pointed out that a child never wins an argument with a parent. The therapy sessions between Natalie and her parents end with accusatory bitterness that eats at Natalie. Natalie maintains the fantasy that all can be repaired if she can be given the normal family history she craves: parents who love her and a home, a place of sanctuary.

The therapy process is bringing back Natalie's self-loathing instead of silencing the noise of guilt in her head. She is no match for her parents. She continues to intrude her struggle to become worthy into every relationship. Her schoolwork is deteriorating again; she is making no effort in courses she needs for college but rather is becoming increasingly abusive toward her teachers. Natalie remains a difficult student in her classes, talkative and disruptive. The teachers who learn to jolly her along and establish a personal relationship win her obedience. However, many teachers cannot do this in their large classes and Natalie becomes intolerable. She has already switched two classes, blaming her problems on deficient teachers. While the school has patience for her behavior, neither the teachers nor the counselors are providing the opportunities and support for Natalie to perform at an acceptable level in preparation for college.

She is also becoming increasingly confrontational and outwardly sexual as if to deny any maturity in rebellion against adult authority. During one choir practice, Natalie claims that she unobtrusively slipped her tank top off underneath a shirt; she insists that she was wearing an athletic bra. The teacher claims that she performed a strip tease. On another day, coming back from class in a schoolbus, the driver reported that she and a number of other girls flashed their breasts at passing motorists. Natalie says this never happened. She was written up for smoking; Natalie says she was simply holding another girl's cigarette. She is becoming more defiant and insolent toward her cottage parents. She cries frequently. She is distraught. She pities herself.

In all her seven years of foster care, Natalie has not encountered a single caretaker who was able, as her cottage mother says, to get into her problems. Her therapists have idealized her, boasting of their savvy insights into her soul. They have identified with her; her first therapist at Camilla Park aggressively projected her own needs back onto Natalie, becoming raucously possessive and weeping piteously when the worried caseworker switched Natalie to another therapist. The different therapists and her many caseworkers have widely different views of Natalie's mother—one claiming she is weak and passive, the other identifying her as the true disciplinarian in the family; one claiming that she is manipulative and charming, the other that she is "dumb as a doornail." They have different interpretations of Natalie's behavior; they tell conflicting stories about her experiences. They see her father differently. Perhaps by way of showing her gratitude for their attentions, Natalie seems to have adeptly reinforced the preferences of her workers, cunningly playing her assigned role in their ponderous melodramas of her life. The therapists adore her for supporting their simplistic explanations of human behavior.

Adam

The worst thought is that in less than two years Adam will graduate from high school. The young man will finally be confirmed as an orphan, dumped into the world without family, relatives, friends, mentors, or even institutional protectors, without savings, adequate schooling, or training, and without the necessary ability to provide for himself. After serving more than thirteen of his eighteen years before the mast of the public child welfare system, he will leave a program as generous as Boys Town without self-discipline, toughness, social grace, the strength to handle reality, or even self-awareness. However, he will leave with his nemesis—a glazed-eyed fury.

Adam is in better shape than many foster children, having had the good fortune to live in an enriched setting for four years. He seems to be a pleasant young man, at least initially. With luck and maturity he might well become a mechanic, even a foreman of mechanics. Like Natalie, his success will probably be a sad one following many unhappy years of futile searches for a place in life. Unfortunately he arrived at Boys Town after absorbing so much abuse that the program probably did little more than provide him respite from the lunacies of his natural mother and the cruelties of his foster parents, who also adopted him.

Adam's mother was a prostitute and drug addict who separated from her husband, Adam's father, one year after his birth. Adam and his mother had no contact with him since then. Adam has been in and out of temporary shelters since the age of two. At that time, Adam was temporarily placed in the youth shelter when his mother was terminated from Aid to Families with Dependent Children (AFDC) and evicted from her apartment. He was reunited with her three months later when she moved in with Adam's grandmother and was able to resume AFDC. Shortly afterward, she moved into an apartment with a man who fathered Douglas then left her six months after he was born. A few months later the boys were placed in a youth shelter when she was jailed for selling drugs. She was convicted and placed on probation.

Shortly after Adam's fifth birthday, a complaint was filed against his mother for abusing drugs and leaving the boys unsupervised at night while she was prostituting herself. Her probation officer made two home visits. During the first visit, the boys were in the care of her live-in boyfriend; the apartment contained adequate food. The boys did not appear to be in imminent danger. During the second visit, the boys' mother was home. She denied allegations of drug use and prostitution but admitted that the living environment was inappropriate for children. The neighborhood was dangerous and transient, hospitable to junkies and prostitutes. There was no play area for the children. The one-bedroom apartment was too small for four people and a dog. She planned to rent a larger apartment in one week and the state took no action to remove the children.

However, a few days later, the live-in boyfriend called the probation officer and reported that the boys' mother left them with him and did not return home the prior evening. He stated that he could no longer care for the boys. The boys were again placed in a shelter.

A few weeks later at the protective custody hearing, Adam's mother reported that she and her boyfriend had separated; without a source of income and a place to live, she could not independently care for her sons. She admitted that her lifestyle was detrimental to her children's welfare. She said that she loved her children and wanted to make the necessary changes to care for them again.

Adam does not remember his father. He does have some recollection of his mother's affections, although the scenes of neglect he also recalls suggest that he may have created the memories as a comfort, a frail memento that he is worth caring for. His case records document a mother driven by addictions and incapacities, confirming Adam's recollections of disordered apartments, loneliness and neglect, malnutrition, and even occasional physical abuse from his mother's lovers and customers. She may have tried to the limits of her capacities to care for her sons, but she failed sorrowfully.

The state placed both Adam and his brother, younger by fifteen months, in a family foster home. Martha and Zachary Bunyon, in their early forties when Adam and his brother arrived, lived in a large wood frame and stucco house on four acres of land isolated in the desert outskirts of Las Vegas. They were zealous, fundamentalist Christians who had four other foster boys in the home in addition to their own two children. They planned to adopt all of the foster children after securing contracts from the state to continue the foster care payments, which averaged about $360 per month for each child, and to provide all of the ancillary services, notably Medicaid, until the children reached their eighteenth birthday. Two of the boys were adopted shortly after Adam and Douglas arrived.[1] Zachary speaks of his cleverness in combining Christian duty and financial security.

Zachary was an intermittent home contractor and had been taking courses toward a bachelor's degree, first at the junior college and then at the university, for the past eleven years. Martha stayed home with the boys and supervised the kennel where the Bunyons raised Dobermans. The Bunyons claimed that the chores around the kennels provided opportunities to teach the boys responsibility and good work habits.

About one and one-half years after Adam and Douglas arrived at the Bunyons, when Adam was almost seven years old, their mother called Martha to relate that she would never be able to take the boys back and that she had made arrangements with the state to give up her parental rights in the hope that the boys might be adopted. She had failed to complete any of the conditions necessary to be reunited with her boys: she did not obtain a job; she was still using drugs and had made no effort to enter a detoxification and treatment program; she had not rented an apartment.

The boys' mother had been visiting them intermittently at the Bunyon home but her behavior had become erratic. She had been arrested again for prostitution and selling drugs. A final meeting was arranged at the state child welfare office for her to say goodbye to Adam and Douglas. Martha called Adam into the living room to tell him about the meeting. She sat him down in a wooden chair under a portrait of Christ and the needlepoint reminder, "God Bless Our Home," to inform him that this would probably be the last time he would see his mother. He began to cry and scream. She told him to grow up and control himself and then left him alone in the living room.

At the meeting, Adam's mother brought him a He-Man comic book as a parting gift. She explained that she was sick and would not be able to see him again. He clutched at her. She kissed him on the cheek, pushed him away, and told him to be a good boy. He never heard from her again. He would like to reach her to ask why she did not stay in touch, not even

---

1. Foster parents are allowed to provide care for as many as six children in Nevada. Adopted children, even if the state continues to provide support, are not counted against this maximum. The Bunyons' decision to adopt was probably also made with this in mind.

a card at Christmastime or a phone call. He feels that he may have been a disappointing son. When he is down on himself, he suspects that he is unspeakably evil.

He was an unruly and attention-seeking child when he started foster care. He was small for his age and although he had an engaging smile and an open face he looked sickly. He fought constantly with the other boys and inflicted pain with little remorse. After his mother abandoned him, he became demonic, almost beyond control, experiencing wide mood swings between aggressive behavior and great sadness. He did poorly in school and was disruptive in his classes. He tested below normal in all academic areas; the school tracked him toward a vocational program. The Bunyons adopted Adam and Douglas about one year after their mother gave up her legal rights.

The Bunyons were strict disciplinarians who responded to the boys' misbehavior in the same physical way that they trained their dogs. However, while they were consistent with the dogs, they never bothered to work out specific rules, rewards, and punishments that the boys might remember. They were quick to verbally and physically penalize any infraction of what they considered to be proper. While the dogs were punished at the point of their misbehavior, the boys could expect days and sometimes weeks of scoldings, slaps, and beatings. Zachary sent a boy to fetch a thick leather belt and then steadied him by the back of his hair for the thrashing. Adam was beaten so often that he stopped crying and simply endured the belt silently, enraging Zachary even further. Adam remembers being kept at home at times by the Bunyons until the welts on the back of his legs and buttocks shrank. He also remembers being redfaced with fury, wishing for the Bunyons to die and fantasizing about how sorry they would be if he died.

The Bunyons assigned Adam the chore of cleaning up the dogs' droppings in their gravel runs. Adam was a lackadaisical worker. One day, Zachary stormed into the house, grabbed Adam by the hair, and pulled him outside. Zachary pushed Adam's face into the ground alongside each pile of dog feces that he had failed to scrape up while screaming at him, "You are no better than this. You are no better than this. . . ."

Martha did not beat the boys with a belt but constantly belittled them, playing one off against the other. The harsh discipline was assisted by Martha's brother. Adam was becoming increasingly defiant. One day Martha's brother grabbed Adam—he was eleven at the time—and dragged him up against the cinder block wall of the garage, yelling into his face, "If you keep giving Martha and Zachary problems, I am going to have you taken care of." He slapped him a few times, shook him, then let him loose.

A few months before he came to Boys Town, Adam disobeyed and cursed Martha. As punishment, the Bunyons locked him in an unfinished, unheated room off the garage for a week. He was allowed out only to use the bathroom, to go to school, and at night to go to bed. Peanut butter and jelly sandwiches were brought to him. During the days Adam was kept there, Zachary dropped by with the other boys to ridicule him for being childish, undisciplined, rude, and mean and to tell him that he wasn't part of the family any more. Adam realized that he was not merely being punished; he was being humiliated. "If I were any bigger, I would've taken out Zachary."

All the boys came to the Bunyon household desperate for acceptance into a family. The Bunyons, however, showed little affection to the foster and adopted children. They were rarely rewarded and even the rewards had a dark, malicious undertone. At times, the Bunyons arbitrarily praised one boy as a standard against which to rebuke another, humiliating both and irritating their relations.

The only other rewards were provided for religious observance—attending services, Sunday school, and weekday prayer meetings—and only when a boy was making active, verbalized progress toward a commitment to Christ in the Bunyons' church. The Bunyons provided opportunities for the church's missionaries to speak with the boys. The church espoused a literalist religion that condemned modernity, holding fiercely to a belief in original sin—the natural tendency of people to be immoral. Parties, television, movies, singing, and dancing were prohibited on Sundays. Country music, however, was allowed. The boys were not permitted stylish haircuts: the white boys were obliged to part their hair in the middle and comb it back; the African Americans were given close-cropped cuts. They were also not permitted any relations with girls outside of school: no calls, no visits, no dates. Coming home after school, the adopted and foster children had to enter the house through the side door.

Every child had a soul that the Bunyons would try to perfect through their church. When warned on occasion by a caseworker not to press his religion on the boys, Zachary whined that he had done nothing wrong, protesting that he was serving God. His proselytizing became furtive but remained relentless.

The Bunyons justified the strict discipline as more than simply teaching self-control and social adaptation. It represented a conscious commitment to moral self-restraint and a realization of the truth of their church's tenets. The Bunyons governed their house under two different sets of rules: one for their own two children and another for the "state" boys. The Bunyons' own children had free access to the toys and bikes donated to the home; they climbed on the counters; they were frequently allowed to plan their own time; their individual rooms were crowded with puzzles, photos, balls, and paints; they were rarely, if ever, corrected or punished. Indeed, they were wild for being undisciplined while the foster and adopted children were wild for being compressed. They were permitted only occasional use of the bikes and toys and only if the Bunyons felt that they were obedient and deserving. The Bunyons did not allow them any personal possessions, and their rooms, each shared by three boys, were barren apart from clothing and school supplies. They were handled roughly and with contempt, raised as though they were monastery acolytes who required mortification to learn discipline, self-denial, and sacrifice. Still, the Bunyons claimed that all the children in their house were treated equally. Yet the foster and adopted children sensed deeply that their struggle for acceptance was futile.

They were given little encouragement to develop their talents, tastes, ideas, and personalities. The Bunyons treated them as uniform targets of religious conversion and unpredictable threats to a reverential, Godly home. Zachary avoided them, particularly the older boys, and relegated the day-to-day chores to his wife. She was not an adept disciplinarian and the boys spoke back to her. When Zachary learned of the insults, he would grab the offending youngster by the neck, shake him, and scream, "No one will disrespect my wife. She is special to me."

One of the foster children was an African American. He was discouraged from learning about black history or socializing with other African Americans. He escaped for a few hours through a side window to see his Big Brother, who provided the only emotional asylum from the Bunyons. In a cold voice, through squinting dislike, Zachary told the youngster that as a punishment, he was to be permanently barred from seeing his Big Brother. The child was devastated. Fortunately, the Big Brother was a police officer who eventually provided a foster home for the boy before he could be adopted by the Bunyons or baptized into their church.

Whatever evening-star epiphany may have called the Bunyons to service in child care was also abetted by their own personal histories and their apparent financial ambitions. Martha's father, a colonel in the United States Army's special services, abandoned the family to remarry when she was seven. Before the desertion, he was rarely home but had become a revered, awe-inspiring hero, adored by his children and his wife. He had won medals both in Korea and in Vietnam, where he had volunteered for two tours of duty. He was killed under suspicious circumstances during a covert operation in the Far East when Martha was seventeen.

As a father and husband, he expected unquestioning compliance with his orders, commanding his family like a platoon. Martha related to her father through her mother's romanticized tales of his valor and service. Her father called her his little princess during their few short discussions. She tried in every way to please him so that he might spend more time with her. She also adored her brother, four years older than she, who took on a paternal role during her father's long absences. They were never confidants but rather soldiers of different rank.

Martha felt vaguely responsible for her father's abandonment of the family and the distance that he maintained from her. She had stiffly envied the popular teenagers in high school, superstitiously accepting her isolation and emotional longing as a just price for her guilt. She had little charm and few friends. Like her mother, she was a plain woman and had been a plain child with stringy blond hair and pale, mottled skin. She sensed that if she were more clever and pretty, she would have been able to win her father's affections.

Martha passed through high school with little distinction and then attended nursing school for two years before quitting to marry Zachary. They met in a church whose sentimental and dated dogma prescribed comforting, idealized roles for both of them. Zachary, like her father, told her what to do and expected her obedience. She accepted him as if he were a hero. She never doubted that her adult role would be one of service and deference to her husband. She did not expect love and was grateful for Zachary's attention and loyalty.

Martha felt helpless to change her destiny. No one had ever liked her enough to encourage her independence and she accepted her dour fate although with some resentment. When she was weak and the Devil influenced her, she was even spiteful.

Zachary had been the middle child of seven, brought up in a small Mississippi town. He enlisted in the army for two years after he graduated from high school. His father worked in a lumber mill and his mother was a cashier in the local supermarket. Neither parent had completed high school and his father read and wrote with difficulty. Life was a drab struggle to keep the children clothed and fed. There was little affection among his weary parents and the children, who were frequently disciplined but largely unsupervised.

His parents were devout members of a fundamentalist sect which was the sole moral authority in their lives. They expressed emotions only during ecstatic services when his mother was often moved to speak in tongues. Their understanding of society and their rules for the children were all predicated on God's expectations, revealed though services, revivals, and the sect's simplified Bible tracts.

By the time that Adam was twelve, after more than six years of humiliation, he had stepped outside the Bunyons' control. The beatings did not intimidate him; he took pride in his tearless pain. He raged uncontrollably back at the taunts, intimidation, and ridicule. He was developing grand illusions about himself as a star athlete, a leader of boys, and a hero, maintaining that at three years old he saved his younger brother from drowning. At school he was on the periphery of youth gangs, enjoying his self-regard as an outlaw. At the same time, he suffered from bouts of immobilizing self-hatred. His inability to escape the Bunyons' judgments recalled his feelings that he had failed his mother.

The Bunyons sought to terminate the adoption. The caseworker found a place at Boys Town for Adam while Douglas, also uncontrollable and growing increasingly violent and psychotic, was sent to a more secure residential treatment center. In return, the Bunyons did not pursue legal termination of their parental rights, even though the adoption was effectively disrupted.[2]

Adam had made little progress with his psychotherapists at the state's Division of Adolescent and Family Mental Health Service (the Division). They considered him to be psychotic. He was finally sent to a competent community psychiatrist and tentatively diagnosed with attention deficit disorder coincidental to manic-depressive disorder. He was put on medication and appeared to calm down enough to adapt to Boys Town.[3] His

2. There are many instances when the rights of adoptive parents are maintained but the child is permanently separated from them. However, these cases are not counted as failed adoptions, and public reports therefore undercount the extent to which the policy emphasis on adoption is misplaced or unwise.

3. Adam continues in the care of the psychiatrist at Boys Town's expense. Boys Town spends its own money to get competent professional care. Las Vegas has few adequate therapists (assuming that psychotherapy is possible to begin with) and Boys Town had made the decision to ensure that Adam continued with a responsible psychiatrist. The state encourages children needing psychotherapy to utilize the therapists of the Division or contract therapists willing to take the state's reimbursements. Some of the Division's therapists have been dropped from more competent staffs and others cannot get hired where professional standards are competitive.

It is also noteworthy that the Division took steps to terminate this case study. Informed consent to participate in the study was initially obtained from Mr. Bunyon (who was Adam's legal guardian in spite of his being at Boys Town), Adam, the state, and Boys Town. When the time came to review Adam's early records with the Division where he had received psychotherapy while he was at the Bunyons' home, the Division made the determination that it would not be in the interests of their patient to disclose the records, even for research purposes. Shortly thereafter, the Division encouraged Mr. Bunyon to retract his permission, claiming that the research was not being ethically conducted. Mr. Bunyon dutifully complied.

It was not clear whether the Division considered Mr. Bunyon or Adam to be its patient. Yet the state's precipitous action raises other issues, most notably the possibility that Mr. and Mrs. Bunyon's abuse was documented in Adam's case records. If this were the case, then the therapists, perhaps believing strongly in their own curative touch, had still failed to comply with their legal obligation to report the abuse. Moreover, the therapists might have felt that the Bunyons were the clients or perhaps the family was the client. In any event, Adam and his brother Douglas were allowed to languish in an appalling adoption with near sadistic adults. Perversely, the Bunyons have been certified recently as therapeutic foster parents, receiving

medication has slowly been reduced over the years. The psychiatrist feels that his rages are situational and that the Division ignored the sadistic abuse that Adam was receiving from the Bunyons. Still, Adam is highly confrontational with episodes of true, glazed-over rage.

Adam has never enjoyed a rite of passage to young adulthood—recognition by at least one special adult of his growth and maturity. He resents the indifference of institutional rules and adult abuse. He is reluctant to distinguish between the Bunyons and his Boys Town cottage parents, fully expecting to be abandoned again and to go through the subsequent bad feelings.

Adam has grown close to his cottage father, an athletic and muscular young man, and an idol along with Michael Jordan for his sports fantasies. But as his need for the affection and approval of the cottage father becomes more apparent to Adam, his fear of losing the relationship also increases and he rages at his misfortune. Three times since he arrived at Boys Town his rage turned inward and he expressed a desire for suicide.

His teachers like him and generally accept his mediocre grades as inherent limitations. He works as a classroom aide for one of the teachers, grading papers, putting them into a computer base, and taking attendance; this is actually a course for which he receives high school credit. He is well behaved at school and ingratiating. One of his teachers refers to him as a "super kid."

Adam is increasingly attracted to gangs, insisting that he has gone through initiation rites in one of them. He has had a number of fistfights during which his rage took control of him. One of the boys at school who apparently owed him ten dollars from a bet "dissed" him in front of others, "Ha, ha, I got your money." Adam punched and slapped him until a teacher pulled him off. He brags of drinking and smoking marijuana.

Since coming to Boys Town he has been working at menial jobs, most recently bagging groceries in a supermarket. He frequently works more

---

about one thousand dollars per month for each terribly disturbed child, similar to Adam and Douglas, that they take into their home.

Perhaps the Division wanted to hide its complicity in this farce. Apparently with the concurrence of the State of Nevada, the Division retains "professional discretion" in making these sorts of decisions without obligation to check its facts or to conform to any fair hearing process. As the state's lawyer argues, "If [the Division] chooses not to cooperate with your study, that is entirely within [its] professional discretion to do so." Imperiousness is not unusual in the public's child welfare system where public functionaries seem besotted with their professionalized wisdom and discretion.

A switch to journalism and frank disclosure in this case would be justice. Yet there is the very reasonable fear among the workers that Adam would simply lose his place at Boys Town as the exposed Bunyons reclaim him to camouflage their abuse.

than twenty hours per week and saves his money. He incants the Boys Town admonition that he learn to work and save, particularly as he will be on his own in two years. But the work is meaningless to Adam, a continuing drudgery of chores and rules broken only by the occasional approval of his adult supervisors. The last time that he called in sick, he simply rode his bike on the streets for hours. He is often sad and despairing, an empty old man in a youth's body.

Boys Town has provided Adam a secure environment but he may not be able to remain there. He lies and rages; he is becoming increasingly competitive and violent toward the other boys, especially at school. His attendance is erratic at work and he occasionally skips school. He is disconnected from his situation and largely disengaged at Boys Town, fantasizing, for example, about becoming an architect. He has not reached a responsible maturity in part because he has been turned into an employee even before he has been a child or a citizen. It is very likely that at the age of eighteen he will join the underground of the public child welfare "disappeareds."

Conclusions

Adam and Natalie have chances for reasonable adult lives but their troubles are hardly over. Boys Town may be the best thing that has happened to them but it came late, after the children had been largely formed through abuse. Many foster kids are far worse off and it would take the most polyannish optimist to accept the foster care system as fair or effective.

Most children in public care have been abandoned—physically and emotionally—by their parents. Many have also been heartlessly abused and neglected. The luckiest child in care is able to attribute the abandonment to specific factors: the death, incarceration, or disease of the parents. The most unfortunate tag themselves with responsibility for their parents' desertions, which they accept as judgments of themselves: unlovely, bad-tempered, and deeply flawed.

Louis Menand stated the problem just so: "Abandonment is the most terrifying circumstance [children] can imagine. . . . It's why children prefer to be securely seated on the lap of a parent when they listen to stories about how marvelous a place the world might be if parents disappeared" (Menand 1997a). The child welfare system takes in frightened and angry children and then continues their abuse and abandonment.

The United States and not simply a few of its depraved parents has turned its back on many of its children. Foster children are not merely abandoned physically and emotionally by their parents but they are outcasts of American society, not worth enough even to justify the costs of minimal criminal and social protection. They had the bad luck to fall into need at a time of remorseless pennypinching.

> I am in a foster home—but still,
> I am not safe. I am being beaten here too.
> "Oh, Dear God, what did I do?"
>
> Natalie

The system actually exacerbates the anger and rebelliousness of the children, whose fury and self-hatred are the natural consequences of being abandoned both by their parents and in effect by society. Their rage, an inescapable noise of self-rebuke, whites out any other experiences, preventing maturation, education, and social learning.

Even when minimal physical safety is secured, the public child welfare system fails to provide them an adequate substitute home, apparently insisting that their impoverished social conditions are carried into their futures. It also fails to handle their emotional deficits either through competent counseling or, when the counseling process is obviously inadequate, through adequate surrogate homes.

Adam was physically and emotionally abused and Natalie was also violated; in these ways both were deprived of the common protections of childhood by their natural parents and then by the public system of care itself. Each suffered from discontinuities in intimacy, absorbing a great amount of malice from their parents followed by the cruelties of the public child welfare system. Adam in particular was also taught violence by sadistic adults who imposed rules without affection or any sense of his distinctiveness. Indeed, for both Natalie and Adam, humiliation in the form of observable degradation was at the center of their punishments.

There is nothing unusual in the stories of Natalie and Adam except perhaps the resilience of these two children and their luck at having come to Boys Town. Hundreds of children are in residential care in southern Nevada. However, many workers feel that perhaps only fifty-five of them are in decent placements—thirty in Boys Town and twenty-five in one other facility. The rest are in the Camilla Parks and the Leisse Homes. It is quietly acknowledged by many close to the system that hundreds more are probably in patently inadequate foster family situations. The Nevada situation is repeated in every other state.

Children internalize abuse which slyly evades their timid defenses, convincing them that they are fundamentally deficient human beings. Foster children bribe their parents with success—improved grades, model friends, shop projects, choral singing, and stylishness and good behavior— to take them home. Against all reason they feel the burden of repairing their damaged parents, hoping to be reinstated in a family, given a respectable identity, and declared normal. Their parents usually do not take them back and the children are embittered by the futility of their emotional negotiations. Worse, many reunions become tragedies.

Perhaps the child welfare system can mark some small achievement in the many behavioral quirks of foster children that fail to reach any standard, treatable criteria of psychiatry's diagnostic manuals. However, their ineligibility for psychiatric protection deprives them of the faint comfort of a categorical pardon and an extended residence in a safe environment. Drafted by a miserly public into its harsh system of care, foster children carry a few worn photos and perhaps a basketball shirt through the doorway of adulthood as offerings to an implacable world.

Adolescence should equip young adults with a sense of mastery, competence, and capacity. These are the tools for a successful adulthood. They are also the pillars of the voluntary associations, attitudes, intelligence, and initiative that construct a vital civic culture and a humane society. Mastery, competence, and capacity require personal mentors to help shape personality and behavior as well as the opportunity to gain confidence in increasing skills, intelligence, and social ability. However, the adults and the situations are denied to foster children. Most notably, the public child welfare system, even at Boys Town, fails to individualize the experiences of family to prepare children for maturity and independence.

Family experiences are very difficult and expensive to re-create. The effects of their provision or deficiency may be measured in diffuse psychological terms. Yet both the material conditions of appropriate family life (opportunities for self-expression and self-testing along with reasonable adults) and the material consequences of their denial (feral children and unsocialized adults, crime, mental disorders, and so forth) are not so speculative and amorphous.

The public child welfare system routinely fails on every level: physical, emotional, educational, and civic. Its meagerness is an instance of social efficiency—cheapening out—not social virtue. The system's conundrums— the catch-22 of improvement, the Peter Principle of foster care, and deferrals of appropriate care—conspire to ensure that its harms are irremedial.

The field's literature, failing to honestly describe the situation of children in care and to evaluate credibly the effects of child welfare programs, is better understood as an architecture of social efficiency than as an advocate for the children. This literature has justified the public child welfare system, allowing even liberals to acquiesce the politics of denial.

2
David Copperfield and the Politics of Care

The American child welfare system has always been inadequate, perhaps as a consequence of the political weakness of its dependents. The culture has spoken eloquently although with quiet embarrassment to the unimportance of these children: an adequate volume of families do not come forward to provide homes for children without parents and many of those who do volunteer need foster care themselves; the public sector fails to allocate sufficient money to underwrite either an adequate surrogate care system or needed supports for families; and, most dispiriting, the literature of child welfare transmits the society's reigning orthodoxies more than the objective reality of the children. In short, children who must rely on the humane impulses of their society cannot count on private volition, public generosity, or the commitment of intellectuals. A just advocacy for the needs of America's David Copperfields has been swamped by the culture's pusillanimous contrivances to save money—its child welfare programs. The contemporary child welfare system, better than any distant mirror, reveals American society without feathers.

The social sciences and the helping professions—the intellectual community for the child welfare system—have assisted the nation to fabricate the exculpating delusion that its grossly underfunded child welfare services are largely sufficient. Social policy relies on the comforting fiction that any deficiencies in the child welfare system will be adequately met by improvements both in the techniques of child care programs and in treatment for behavioral problems as well as through redefinitions of the problem itself. In this way, child welfare programs with novel claims to "proven capacity" have been enthusiastically implemented: to select and train more proficient foster parents, to effectively counsel and treat disturbed children, to provide appropriate protections for children in placement, and to prevent family dissolutions that result in more expensive reliance on relatively long-term child welfare placements. At the same time, the intellectual community has endorsed the taxpayer's natural preference to reduce the public commitment to deprived children by periodically insisting that child wel-

31

fare services can be restricted to a relatively small population of truly needy children to minimize the number of placements.

However, all of the claims for the adequacy of minimal social welfare provisions—the notion that the child welfare system can realize socially efficient goals—have failed the test of time as well as more rigorous appraisals. There has never been any credible demonstration that budgetary minimalism has succeeded in child welfare. Programs for dependent children routinely fail to achieve their goals. The porous research prevents any conclusions except indeterminacy and failure. The advertised successes are the bulletins of changing social attitudes and the hucksterism for emerging fashions in compassion more than serious attempts to interrupt social problems.

The failure to design effective social interventions for dependent children stems largely from the inability of minimal programs—particularly foster family care and most residential group settings—to compensate for serious cultural deprivation. Children's emotional, material, psychological, and social deficits result from disrupted and inadequate participation in the basic institutions of the American culture, most notably the family, the community, and the educational system. The failures of these institutions to socialize children are likely to be expressed graphically in crime, mental and physical disease, poverty, out-of-wedlock childbearing, school failure, and the wide range of inappropriate and oppositional social behaviors that impair the civic culture.

The child welfare caseload is probably not isolated from the fortunes of the general population but instead may well be the most extreme and frank evidence of the inadequacies of the culture. In 1994, the child welfare system provided direct services to about 700,000 children whose natural families refused or were unable to care for them. Each year as many as 1.8 million children come to the attention of investigators through complaints of neglect or abuse. A few hundred thousand of these complaints eventuate in child welfare placements. Yet there is probably an even larger number of American children whose futures are seriously clouded by inadequate participation in critical social institutions but who are not enumerated among the maltreated and therefore fail to increase consciousness of the extent of social problems. In comparison with other modern industrial societies, the United States has shouldered little public responsibility for social failure, particularly in reference to the welfare of children (Rainwater and Smeeding 1995).

The politics of American child welfare typically depreciate both need and the response to need. Indeed, the recent period of child welfare programs—dating from Maas and Engler's (1959) classic statement of the failure of foster care—and probably much of American social welfare history can be understood as taking a short-term profit from the denial of social reality.

American society provides a powerful incentive to contrive definitions of both social need and social response that acquiesce to the orthodoxy of social efficiency. Yet these myths carry their own perils as social conditions may become pathologically infectious. The tension between denial and threat bracket the social dialectics of public welfare: contemporary policy chooses to address deep cultural deprivation with only minimal interventions and at minimal cost even while inadequate policy threatens the first-order social priorities to maintain order and to promote harmony.

In this sense the scholarly literature of child welfare composes parables for the contemporary policy debate—the studies that purport to offer effective child welfare programs—that have an important influence over the destiny of many children. Unfortunately, the literature has failed to provide children with either a strong advocacy or an accurate characterization of their needs. In the end, it has justified neglect.

Child welfare programs tend to be fashionably enthusiastic more than objective. As the market for solutions to social problems heats up, the intellectual community is enticed to tender programs even while evidence of their effectiveness is stubbornly indeterminate. Hopeful leads such as psychotherapeutic counseling programs and family preservation serve a political function in satisfying the culture's demand for symbols of charitability. However, they fail to address their defining problems.

The professional rewards for creating satisfying symbols have overwhelmed the scientific safeguards of the community of child welfare scholars. As a result, studies of child welfare programs are routinely among the weakest research in the social sciences. Statements of program outcomes are not credible. Characterizations of problems are suspect. Even simple descriptions of the child welfare system are customarily incomplete. While some of the inaccuracy results from inadequate resources, the distortions of the research raise questions about the commitments of the field and the motives of its auspices. Indeed, child welfare research is plagued by the ideological blinders of the right and the left, principally the promise to be able to correct the defining problems of child welfare with relatively inexpensive interventions that are compatible with current institutional arrangements. This commitment to social efficiency has even distorted analyses that seat the problem of child welfare in the United States' structural insufficiencies, notably economic poverty and racism.

In addition to its ideological bias, the research has also routinely failed to credibly identify the causes of family dysfunction, children's problems, placement decisions, or the outcomes of care. Child welfare interventions have never been credibly evaluated. Even the most sophisticated research—

for example, the evaluation of family preservation in Illinois—is beset by so many methodological problems that its findings are indeterminate at best. As a result, no reasonable estimates of program effectiveness are possible. More troubling, the indeterminacy of outcomes abets the largely ideological discussion of child welfare.

With a startling uniformity, the research has avoided evaluating the most critical outcomes of child welfare services. Hardly any program is evaluated against the actual conditions of the child. Almost every study assumes that placement dispositions—reunification with natural parents, adoption, long-term family foster care, institutional or congregate care, and so forth—sufficiently capture the interests of the child. With rare exceptions, and even these are problematic, the literature cannot describe the effects of child welfare placements on the emotional, mental, physical, social, or educational progress of the child. It is obvious that the attentions of researchers are monopolized by strong social preferences to define child welfare as a budgetary problem for the public sector rather than as a problem of cultural deprivation for the child.

The presumption that reunification with natural parents and adoption are desirable is a canard unless evidence can be adduced that the child does better in relatively permanent situations than in alternative placements, namely, long-term foster care of one sort or another. In this sense, then, the various defining problems and goals of the child welfare system—drift, bounce, neglect, permanency, reunification, preservation, and so forth—are ascriptions of dominant social preferences rather than reflections of social reality, that is, the actual conditions of the children at risk.

The "child's best interest" is a highly contentious notion that has caromed back and forth between the rights of parents and the rights of children. A cost-conscious society obviously learns to tolerate the vagaries of diverse child-rearing practices. A more humane and ambitious society might sacrifice some amount of personal liberty in the interests of greater rights to standardized and more generous conditions of citizenship.

At each epoch of child welfare in contemporary America, a unique form of neglect has been fashioned with the connivance of the intellectual community to justify a minimal public provision for child welfare. With little if any evidence of its impact on the children, the central pressure since even before Maas and Engler (1959) has been to empty the public child welfare system either by preventing placements or through adoption and reunification with parents; the actual experience of the children has been largely ignored. The experiments that endorsed the Adoption Assistance and Child Welfare Act of 1980 (Act of 1980), a legislative milestone in American child welfare, spoke with a near uniform voice to the possibility for more efficiently handling intake, for improving treatment, and for better placements. And all this could be achieved while actually saving money or only at minimal cost.

The Act of 1980 also championed family preservation, the notion that short-term and relatively inexpensive services could prevent extensive reliance on the child welfare system by repairing troubled families in order to prevent their dissolution. The fundamental assumptions of these interventions test the modern practice of the professions of helping, their ability to explain social dynamics and to design interventions to improve functioning. Both of these assumptions are outgrowths of social science promises to apply rational analysis to problems of living. Unfortunately, the failure of family preservation services, typical of the failures of therapeutic human services generally, suggests that the scientific practice of social understanding is freighted by perhaps insurmountable obstacles. The possibility of social engineering has still not been demonstrated.

Alternative approaches to successfully socialize children are still politically unpopular. American society has refused to ensure greater cultural parity for children by attacking the problems of economic poverty and cultural deprivation. Yet the relationship among economic poverty, cultural deprivation, and human behavior remains unclear. Some families and children would undeniably benefit from the greater availability of day care, housing, employment, and other concrete supports. Nevertheless, the problems of the largest proportion of families who cannot or will not or should not be permitted to raise children will probably persist in spite of the simple provision of economic or concrete resources. Many dysfunctional parents, perhaps themselves the products of deficient experiences in family, community, and school will probably never be made whole; psychotherapy and other minimal interventions have failed to dispel the skepticism that human behavior once formed is doggedly resistant to change.

In contrast with the minimal efforts, the bill to provide the underlying protections and resources to guarantee cultural parity—families, communities, and schools that provide at least minimally acceptable experiences— is vastly greater than the amount needed simply to ensure that the income gaps which define economic poverty, especially at the low American poverty line, are partially filled. The amount necessary to substantially reduce cultural deficits appears to be beyond current political consideration. Nevertheless, the refusal to allocate an adequate amount for child welfare services is not the result of the nation's financial incapacity. Rather, the austerity of public child welfare has come about because of a weak political will, particularly appalling in consideration of the relatively few children who come into the child welfare system.

Ideology and Child Welfare Services

The largest portion of child welfare scholarship is strongly influenced by modern liberalism and its preference for structural rather than genetic, individual, or subcultural explanations for social failure. As it affects social welfare, liberalism holds that the poor are largely similar to the nonpoor (Danziger, Sandefur, and Weinberg 1994; Edin 1995; Edin and Lien 1997; Gans 1995; Rank 1994). Economists have tried mightily to show that the motives that govern the nonpoor—labor force participation and family formation, for example—also govern the poor (Danziger, Sandefur, and Weinberg 1994; Ellwood and Bane 1985; Moffitt 1992). If there are no telling personal differences between the different socioeconomic classes, then the poor are the random victims of unfortunate social conditions such as the death or abandonment of a spouse, unemployment, bad parents, and inadequate schools, or the targeted victims of injustices such as racism or sexism. In this sense, if poverty results from society's imperfections, then the poor are not responsible for their poverty and therefore have legitimate claims on public relief. Liberals have been loath to acknowledge any subcultural or personal factors that distinguish the poor from the nonpoor and that might derive their economic predicament from moral or characterological choices for which they are personally responsible.

In the face of evidence that there may be distinguishing personal factors that differentiate the poor from the nonpoor—such as the absence of impulse control, promiscuity, alcoholism and drug addiction, sloth, impertinence and oppositional attitudes, an absence of personal hygiene, a lack of initiative, inattention, low school attendance, a propensity for violence, intellectual incapacity, ignorance, and stupidity—liberal thought still insists that social conditions cause individual and group deviations.[1] Thus individual shortcomings result from an absence of free will, not inappropriate personal choices; in this way the stress that naturally attends conditions of economic deprivation causes individual deviance. Taking the logic another step, liberals claim that invoking personal irresponsibility as an excuse to withhold welfare constitutes the injustice of blaming the victim.

On their part, conservatives minimize the effects of structural impediments, arguing that individuals are responsible for themselves. Therefore, people need to be held accountable by enduring the consequences of their choices such as poverty, low status, and even bad health. Conservatives have consistently pressed for a reduction of public support, reluctantly accepting responsibility for only a small caseload of dependents—children or

---

1. A large literature notes many differences between the poor and nonpoor in social attitudes and behaviors. See Epstein (1997:224 n.1).

adults—and only for the most frozen objectives. Philanthropy—the charitable action of the private sector—is a sufficient corrective for any inadvertent imperfections in the working of the marketplace.

Nevertheless, the nature of the relationship between poverty and child welfare placements remains elusive. While the association between poverty and various indicators of social problems seems to be strong, the causative relationship between them is nearly impossible to establish. Does poverty provoke drug addiction, for example, a factor that Wulczyn (1994) presents in explanation of the enormous increase in infant placements in New York City between 1985 and 1989? Or is poverty the logical consequence of drug addiction and of the personal and subcultural choices that may lead to drug addiction? The problem of child welfare is approached differently depending on which alternative—structural factors or the constellation of personal and subcultural influences—in fact causes and sustains the poverty.

The typical liberal welfare package contains targeted personal social services, minimal income transfers, and some form of job support strategy such as training. Yet unless structural factors—the absence of money and not the dysfunctional behaviors of the parents—are the principal influences over family dissolution, the reduction of poverty will have little influence over the need for child welfare. Moreover, liberal thought has not come to grips with the intransigence of social problems and the relative superficiality of its preferred interventions. Simply mimicking a few material conditions of the nonpoor may not be sufficient to induce conforming behavior. In contrast, the conservative position reduces to a policy of willful neglect, a barbarity, unless it is wise to allow children to invent themselves, *pace Lord of the Flies,* and then hold them responsible for their own socialization.

Pelton (1989, 1994), a social worker and an avowed liberal, exemplifies the intellectual transformation of the needs of maltreated children into morsels of professionalization and a confederacy of trivial programs. He argues that many more families can be preserved and many more foster children can be reunited with their families by resolving the child welfare workers conflicting responsibilities and by simply redirecting the expenditure of existing child welfare resources from the treatment and care of foster children to concrete services for their natural families. Thus the enduring conundrums of child welfare dissolve into relatively congenial tasks of professional technique and programmatic design that remain largely within existing budgets.

Pelton (1989) asserts that a "dual role" circumscribes the effectiveness of child welfare workers. The role conflict is created when workers have responsibilities for both policing reportedly maltreating parents and offering

them services. Pelton argues that by relieving the workers of their puni-
tive functions, their effectiveness in providing services will greatly improve.
Nevertheless, it seems fanciful to focus on professional role conflicts when
the amount of unmet need is so great; when the literature has failed even
under optimal conditions to credibly demonstrate any return for modestly
funded and underfunded psychosocial interventions; and when the surveillance of maltreating families may be the only benefit of family preservation
and reunification services.

Pelton defines poverty principally as "material hardship" and argues
that it is the root cause of failed families; maltreatment is a minor problem.
Therefore, he proposes a range of concrete services—day care, respite, income assistance, housing and so forth—to prevent many if not most family
dissolutions that result from abandonment and neglect. Furthermore, by
reducing the daily frustrations of low income through concrete services,
far fewer children will be abused. Pelton has read through the literature
exhaustively but with a directed finger in order to claim that the research
supports both his structural analysis of the causes of placement and the
effectiveness of his solutions.

> There is overwhelming and remarkably consistent evidence—across a
> variety of definitions and methodologies and from studies performed
> at different times—that poverty and low income are strongly related to
> child abuse and neglect and to the severity of child maltreatment. Chil-
> dren from impoverished and low-income families are vastly overrepre-
> sented in the incidence of child abuse and neglect. The strong relation-
> ship between poverty and low income and child abuse and neglect holds
> not only for child abuse and neglect in general but for every identified
> form of child abuse and neglect, including emotional abuse, emotional
> neglect, and sexual abuse. (Pelton 1994:167)

However, Pelton's simplistic structural theory of the causes of social
failure, in moralistic and stern denial of any entrenched behavioral differences that distinguish the poor from the nonpoor, has never been credibly
verified. The belief that only superficial differences distinguish socioeconomic classes in the United States naturally endorses comforting and inexpensive policy proposals such as Pelton's ambition to divert child welfare
moneys from long-term care to concrete services. These sorts of proposals and theories tend to cheapen the problems of poverty by avoiding any
deep scrutiny of the American social system itself. Yet correlation is not
cause, and even if Pelton's studies were able to conclude convincingly that
poverty as material deficit is the principal cause of family failure, they have
still identified neither the determinants of poverty itself nor effective points
of intervention.

No study has demonstrated that modestly raising income or easing material hardship has the effect of improving family functioning. To the contrary and in defiance of liberal dogma, the line of causation may often run from behavioral problems (addiction, violence, impulsiveness) to an inability to secure adequate income. Indeed, Mayer (1997) is laying claim to academic fame by an attempt to establish the moral roots of good parenting, even among the poor. Subcultural presumptions are usually plausible precursors for structural factors. Thus initial cause becomes an arbitrary point of regression in an endless link chain of personal behavior and structural conditions. In short, the causes of social failure, including poverty, have defied rational testing while the body of research cannot sustain the heightened value of concrete services over behaviorally oriented interventions such as counseling and psychotherapy.[2] It is becoming clearer that very little is known about "welfare as we know it" (Epstein 1997).

The effort to explain the burgeoning child welfare system is part of the more general political contest over the provision of public welfare, the issue of whose claims should be satisfied through public policy. The identification of the cause of the increased child welfare system naturally implies specific types of interventions. Obviously, poverty as a reason for family failure is attractive to those who wish to increase income transfers. In contrast, character failure, perhaps expressed as drug addiction, unemployment, or long-term welfare dependence, offers a reason to deny public funds to afflicted groups and to deal in a cursory fashion with their children.

Similarly, any remedy for the large number of dependent children in long-term public care can logically seek to address the factors that cause the need for placement in the first place—the structural imperfections of both American society and the child welfare system or the personal and subcultural incapacities of the natural parents. If, for example, drug and alcohol addiction precipitate the need for child placement, then treatment programs would seem to be indicated. If economic poverty, however, is associated both with placement and with other complicating conditions such as addiction, then relief of economic insufficiency would also have to be added into any strategy to prevent placement or to restore families. Yet if the decision to take children away from their parents seems to be a professional preference of child care workers perhaps reflecting their utopian commitments or simply their arbitrary sense of the suitability of the natural parents, then the system itself needs to be reformed.

However, the basic reasons for social failure need not be addressed.

2. The same argument extends with considerable force into all of the social services—concrete and psychotherapeutic—notably including interventions focused on poverty and welfare (Epstein 1993a, 1995).

Rather, interventions can pragmatically attempt to mitigate the sustaining causes of any social problem. Through trial and error, social programs that offer promise of achieving consensus goals such as a reduction of the long-term child welfare caseload can be developed and tested.

Yet whether the initial justification for a social intervention is deeply theoretical or naively practical, a very factional, partisan debate surrounds the desirability of these different remedies. Even apart from the very elusive issue of programmatic effectiveness, each remedy implies different rewards and penalties for different groups of people. Different political interests commit to different causes. Simplistically, taxpayers benefit from minimal public solutions while the poor benefit from income transfers intended to preserve families.[3] In a similar fashion, minimal approaches to the foster care problem—say, drug rehabilitation for natural parents, higher thresholds for defining abuse and neglect, and long-term family foster care—better serve conservative family rights interests than a lavish system of group homes and expensive prevention efforts. Thus both the causes of the child welfare system's increase and the implied solutions are politically sensitive.

All solutions would at least appear to be grounded in the issue of effectiveness. Unfortunately, there has been no credible demonstration of any program's effectiveness in reducing child welfare caseloads, in successfully restoring broken families, in treating troubled youngsters, or in preventing placements to begin with. To the contrary, the most credible research, such as it is, suggests that child welfare interventions are ineffective. At the same time, and for many of the same reasons, there is no credible identification of the factors—either the initial causes or the mediating, sustaining causes—that precipitate the needs for long-term care. At an even more rudimentary level, there is no reasonably accurate picture of the needs of the children in care or their progress through care. As a result, no program appears to have worked while the policy-making process appears to be baffled by the most fundamental questions of what to do.

The failure to design effective programs thwarts the ability to finesse political conflict through pragmatic solutions and drives social dialectics back to the difficult theoretical consideration of cause. To the extent to which cause has not been credibly identified or cannot be defined, the political debate becomes increasingly ideological, freed from any rational

---

3. It is usually less expensive to treat a condition than to prevent it, especially when the population at risk cannot be defined or is enormous. Few of the poor become deeply delinquent, yet tens of millions are at risk. The cost for jails while seemingly huge is a tidbit compared to annual budgetary costs for providing greater economic and social parity (assuming for the moment that crime is not determined genetically).

grounding. Indeed, political stakes explain the current child welfare system more accurately than concern with children's benefits.

Low public expenditure as a popular ideology has created incentives for inexpensive remedies to the foster care problem. A taxpayer's logic insists that the high out-of-home caseload results from mistakenly rigorous criteria for maltreatment (including the witch-hunt for sexual abuse) as well as from the refusal to expedite alternatives such as adoption and family reunification as remedies for expensive public care. Liberals have reinforced this position through the child welfare literature, a shameless accommodation to the triumph of contemporary conservative social policy in its inadequate provisions for needy children.

The Child Welfare System

The typical pathway into the child welfare system begins with the report of child maltreatment, that is, abuse or neglect or both. The maltreatment report triggers an investigation, usually by child protection authorities or the police. The number of maltreatment reports has tripled since the enactment of the Child Abuse Prevention and Treatment Act of 1974, which mandated child maltreatment reports by a variety of professionals, notably teachers and physicians.

In 1993, there were approximately 2.5 million reports on individual children, a rate of 43 reports per 1,000 children.[4] Almost 40 percent of the maltreatment reports were supported by investigation, which implies that 3.4 American children per 1,000 were abused physically, 6.9 per 1,000 were neglected, and 2.0 per 1,000 were sexually abused. Most disturbing, only about half of the actual child maltreatment may be reported (Costin, Karger, and Stoesz 1996).

The investigation of a maltreatment complaint leads to dismissed charges, temporary emergency services, or both emergency services and referral to ongoing care. In turn, ongoing care, typically mediated through a court proceeding, results either in return home, frequently with supervision and services to forestall future maltreatment, or relatively permanent substitute care in family foster homes, with relatives (i.e., kinship care) or in a variety of group homes. Moreover, some children are adopted and others are placed in formal guardianship arrangements.

General attention to the child welfare system has increased as a consequence of the precipitous rise in out-of-home placements since the mideighties. Rising from less than one billion dollars in 1985 to about four

4. Except when otherwise noted, data that describe the public child welfare system are from Committee on Ways and Means (1996:chapter 12).

billion dollars in 1995, federal costs have increased greatly to fund more child welfare workers, child welfare agencies, and maintenance stipends. In 1994, some 698,000 children received substitute care in the United States; about 469,000 of these children received family foster care, the largest substitute care program. At the start of 1994, approximately 444,000 children were in out-of-home placements, representing an increase of nearly two-thirds since 1982. Approximately one-third of 1994 placements were placed with relatives.

Reflecting the distribution of substantiated complaints, about half of the children enter foster care because of maltreatment and about half for other reasons such as the physical or mental illness of parents or their incarceration. When children exit from care, about two-thirds of the children are reunified with their parents, about 7 percent age out of the system, about 8 percent are adopted, and the remainder marry, run away, go to prison, or are discharged to another agency. A sizable portion of the caseload is given long-term guardianships. A small percentage are simply lost to the system and cannot be accounted for. Public concern focuses on the apparently large number of children who remain in care. The proportion of this population of children who *should* be in permanent placements — those who are "adrift" in care and those who "bounce" from placement to placement — has been an issue of considerable debate over the years.

The recent increase in the size of the child welfare system has been largely explained by an increased number of children coming into care (including reentries from failed adoptions and reunifications) and a declining exit rate from care rather than by increasing lengths of stay in care (Tatara 1994; Wulczyn 1991; Wulczyn and Goerge 1992). At least over the four years (1985–88) of Tatara's study, median lengths of stay for those who exited care averaged about eight months while those who remained in care averaged one and one half years. Yet Tatara's rigorous description of the dynamics of the child welfare system fails to identify the explanatory factors.

Drawing more upon his schooled imagination than on the research itself, Tatara offers a series of plausible reasons for the increase — more debilitated children, greater difficulty of family reunification, more demanding criteria for reunification, along with a series of structural reasons — while delicately suggesting that "these factors have not been validated through empirical research" (1994:139). Nevertheless, he concludes that the fundamental reasons for family failure and the consequent need to rely on child welfare services are "deeply rooted in very difficult societal problems (e.g., poverty, joblessness, inadequate housing, poor education)" (142). Yet in reaching this conclusion he also questions the priorities of the child welfare system, in particular, the issue of whether more placements could be prevented by emphasizing services to natural parents. Recalling Pelton, the curious logic that pairs structural explanations for placement with weak case service remedies is characteristic of the rhetoric of child welfare reform. A sizable research effort has been made over the past few decades to identify the specific reasons, apart from an obvious public concern with child maltreatment, for the persistence and then, beginning in the mid-1980s, the large rise in the long-term child welfare caseload. This goal has also implied an attempt to explain the duration of child welfare placements. The ability to explain the utilization of child welfare services is part of a broader strategy to develop specific programs that either prevent placement or reduce the time spent in placement. Presumably, service strategies can be developed to handle the factors associated with placement and placement duration. Yet, while the measurement of length of stay in care has been difficult, the identification of explanatory factors has been even more conflicted and problematic.

Explaining the Utilization of Child Welfare Services

Researchers have pointed out that the reemergence of child maltreatment as a social concern in the late 1960s caused a great increase in the child welfare caseload. They have attributed the rise in the complaints that drive the size of the child welfare caseload to many factors: an actual increase in maltreatment (although this rarely is argued explicitly), Kempe et al.'s (1962) identification of the child abuse syndrome, a prurient public fascination with child sexual abuse, the rise of the women's rights movement, and others, notably including a social policy preference for restricting services to a relatively small number of the maltreated rather than the much larger group of those at risk. The provision of care for maltreated children, by creating an organizational and professional stake in those services, has also been implicated in the caseload increase (Stein and Gambrill 1985). The suspicion is often voiced that social workers may keep children in care to protect their jobs. The 1974 legislation, strengthened in subsequent modifications to authorize social services for abused and neglected children, employed a public health logic to mandate the reporting of child maltreatment (Costin, Karger, and Stoesz 1996).

Lindsey (1994) argues firmly that child maltreatment and its attendant services are red herrings to divert attention from the underlying social conditions that create most of the true needs for placement. As a consequence of widespread attention to abuse and neglect, the system's preciously scarce resources have been diverted from services for parents that would facilitate reunification and prevent placement in the first place to efforts to investigate and provide service for abused children. Much of the literature persistently holds the view that many children in foster care and youth shelters are inappropriately removed from their parents.

However, inappropriate removal has not been tested by any systematic evaluation of the children or their parents. Indeed, the absence of any rigorous or consistent standards for placement has fueled suspicions that children are arbitrarily and routinely brought into the child welfare system (Emlen et al. 1976; Pelton 1989; Stein and Gambrill 1985; Stein and Rzepnicki 1983; Wald 1975, 1976). Nevertheless, a number of factors mitigate the likelihood of capricious removal. The American public has become extraordinarily sensitive to costs and government seems loath to incur any additional obligations. Rather than capricious removal, the argument seems more plausible that too many children are left in dangerous situations with abusing parents. After all, between 25 percent and 50 percent of parents who murder their youngsters have been or currently are under the supervision of child welfare authorities (Costin, Karger, and Stoesz 1996).

Maas and Engler's seminal project (1959) studied children in foster care during eleven months. Their alarming findings suggested that many children drifted for years through foster care limbo, bouncing from one placement to another without being reunited with their parents or settled in permanent settings, preferably through adoption. The median length of stay for their sample of 551 children who remained in foster care was 3 years. Among the 882 children who left foster care during the study, those who were adopted had been in care for 1.2 median year, those who returned home had been in care for 1.0 median years, and those leaving for other reasons (e.g., aging out of the system) had been in care for fully 6.0 median years. Moreover, only about one-third of the children had a single placement while about one quarter had been in four or more placements. They also reported that parental visits to children in foster care were important determinants of eventual family reunification.

Focusing largely on the administrative and legal impediments to permanency, Maas and Engler's research, however, was quite limited, more like a series of case studies than an attempt to characterize child welfare services nationally; it drew cases from only nine communities and handled them largely as unique sites.[5] Moreover, the authors arbitrarily eliminated from their sample all children who had been in placement for less than three months, thus exaggerating their reported lengths of stay. On the other hand, their tabulations of lengths of stay for those in care naturally

5. There could be no assurance that their sample was in any way representative of the nation, although it did conform in many ways with Jeter's (1963) sample.

underestimated the true durations which had still not ended (a problem of right-hand censoring).

The then contemporary cross-sectional research which shared Maas and Engler's limitations also tended to support their findings (Bryce and Ehlert 1971; Jeter 1963; Knitzer, Allen, and McGowan 1978; Maas 1969; Magura 1981; Vasaly 1976).[6] However, the longitudinal research that included all recipients of foster care over time and that was conducted during a similar period better characterizes the true role of foster care. The longitudinal research reported considerably less drift and bounce. Jenkins (1967) also included short-term placements; she found that fully 54 percent left care within the first three months and 75 percent left care within two years. Similar, relatively short lengths of stay were also reported by others (Lawder, Poulin, and Andrews 1986; Magura 1979; Testa 1985; and others).[7] Moreover, both Pardek (1984) and Fanshel and Shinn (1978) found that approximately three-quarters of the children in foster care experienced only one or two placements, suggesting far less bounce than Maas and Engler.

Nevertheless, Maas and Engler's findings and especially the recommendations appended to their study, which were written by Joseph H. Reid of the Child Welfare League of America, gave an enormous boost to the permanency planning movement. The perspective of the recommendations inspired a series of service experiments, evaluated in the next chapter, that influenced the content and passage of the Act of 1980. Reid suggested that appropriate social services could prevent placement to begin with while a more aggressive legal strategy might facilitate adoption for the many children whose parents had abandoned them without severing legal ties. He also guessed that there were many more families who would be available to adopt foster children if agencies stepped up efforts to identify them. Reid

6. Jeter (1963) in particular recognized the problem of characterizing a system by point-in-time data. The one-day census "assumes of course that the universe is measured by the total count of children on one day of the year. Actually a larger and different universe might be counted by including all children who pass through the hands of an agency during an entire year" (160). In the end, Jeter's findings tend to corroborate the studies that report far less duration in care than Maas and Engler.

7. Fanshel and Shinn's (1978) longitudinal study tended to support Maas and Engler's longer lengths of stay. Although they did not compute actual duration, 36.4 percent of their sample were still in care five years after entry. However, Fanshel and Shinn also restricted their sample to those in placement for at least ninety days and only selected children up to twelve years of age who had never been in care before and who came into care only during a single year, 1966. They also ignored those placed for adoption. While right-hand censoring would tend to depress the lengths of stay in their sample, its other restrictions exaggerate estimates of long-stayers.

also recommended increased use of group homes for long-term foster care children and encouraged parental visits to their children in foster care to accelerate early family reunification. Some years later, Fanshel and Shinn (1978), Lawder, Poulin, and Andrews (1986), Pine, Warsh, and Maluccio (1993), Davis et al. (1996), and notably McMurtry and Lie (1992) made much of the value of parental visits in shortening duration in foster care and in realizing the goals of permanency planning.

> In order to keep families intact, every community must provide a wide range of service, including financial assistance, marital counseling, psychiatric services, homemaker service, day care, and many other social services that are as necessary as a clean water supply in every American community. In the broader sense, the only preventive for children having to live unnecessarily in foster care is a healthy, economically prosperous, morally strong American family and a healthy, prosperous, and morally strong community. . . . We need not wait upon research to discover, however, how large a percentage of children would not be in care were basic services available in every community. Among the services most frequently absent in the American community are those designed to identify early the family that is in trouble and to bring services to it. (Maas and Engler 1959:381–82)

Reid's residual but still structural approach to child welfare problems, along with his structural assumptions about cause, has echoed through the past few decades but in much diminished form both in appropriations for legislated programs and within the child welfare literature. However, the same problems—the inadequacy of substitute care and the inability to target services on families at risk—persist. Although his strategy largely gives up on reunification, the more recent failure of family preservation has once again revitalized interest in services to move children more quickly out of substitute care and preferably back to their families. However, recommendations subsequent to Reid, while sharing his general goals, are pointedly silent on providing "healthy, economically prosperous" families, preferring instead to follow his service strategy albeit at seemingly less intense levels of care.

Benedict and White (1991) support earlier longitudinal estimates that the duration of care for the largest portion of the caseload is rather short; between 1980 and 1983 only about one-quarter of their sample of Maryland foster children remained in care longer than two years. Moreover, longer stays in care were associated with expected personal problems—the children's poor health, lagging development, and inadequate school performance along with the mother's health problems, notably including alcoholism. Curiously Benedict and White do not find significant associations between length of stay on the one hand and mental health and behavior problems on the other. Yet as the authors point out in a comprehensive review of the literature, contradictory findings in explaining duration are characteristic of the literature. Indeed, these contradictions would seem to be actually generated by a literature that typically addresses only regional experiences and employs an enormous variety of weak methodologies.

Lawder, Poulin, and Andrews (1986), who largely corroborate Benedict and White, also find that the child's behavioral problems are characteristically associated with longer placements. Magura (1979), Fanshel (1976, 1979), Finch, Fanshel, and Grundy (1986), and others, report inconsistent findings about age as a predictor of duration.

Finch, Fanshel, and Grundy (1986), studying the cases of more than twenty thousand New York City children still in care at the end of 1974, report that those in foster care who were adopted differed from those who were discharged to their parents, who remained in care, or who left the system for other reasons. The research compared children who were "adoptive" (designated as ready for adoption) with all others. The study's "child structural variables"—years in care, age at entry, whether the child is legally free for adoption, discharge objective, and whether the child's family was receiving services—best predicted discharge.

> Increased length of time in care was associated with a lower probability of discharge for both adoptive and nonadoptive children. Children who were older were less likely to be discharged. For adoptive children, being freed for adoption was associated with a lower probability of being adopted. For nonadoptive children, the child's discharge objective of being returned to parents or relatives was associated with a greater probability of being discharged in this way, while the family's receipt of services was associated with a lower probability of being so discharged. (Finch, Fanshel, and Grundy 1986:17)

Seaberg and Tolley (1986) expand on the number of descriptive variables in prior research in predicting 40 percent of the variance in the duration of foster care, a modest amount of explanation but still more than other studies. However, whether their ability to describe 40 percent of the variance is an indictment of the child welfare system for its irrationality—the failure to identify objectively the justifications for discharges—or whether it is simply a commentary on the immature state of the research itself is debatable. Still, the findings emerge precariously from limited, conflicting research while

> a profile seems to emerge. On the one hand, a child will spend a longer time in foster care if one or more of the following conditions describe his or her case: the child was abandoned; the child is physically or men-

tally impaired; the child is older, black, or male; adoption services are being provided; and the caseworker has many years of experience. On the other hand, a child will spend a shorter time in foster care when the child is in care for reasons of abuse, parent–child relationship problems or officially deviant behavior; when strengthening the family is a goal of service; when emergency care and protective services are provided; when parental contact with the child continues; and when the caseworker's educational background is in social work. (Seaberg and Tolley 1986:17)

These conclusions may be quite reasonable, describing nearly intractable problems that require major additional resources if they are to be resolved or prevented. Cases designated as amenable for reunification may have been, in truth, disposed in this way because of the parents' temporary problems, such as illness or incarceration. On the other hand, when placement was not due to temporary conditions, reunification and adoption may have been very difficult to achieve. In this way, parents who received services may have been less able to care for their children. Parents who do not visit their children may be trying to abandon them further, and coerced visitations will probably not improve their feelings but may further harm the child. The findings may simply be testifying to the bleak chances of success for either prevention or reunification through the provision of weak and largely temporary social services for parents.

Yet while the findings may be accurate descriptions of the state of foster care, they provide no prescription for policy. The research cannot disentangle cause and effect; simply proving that research findings are accurate and that its samples are representative is problematic. For example, the likelihood that African American children may experience longer durations in foster care does not by itself separate out the reasons: more debilitated parents, fewer adoptive possibilities, caseworker neglect, court preferences, racism, or some combination.[8] Even so, correlations are often pressed as evidence to support the replication, usually through services or case management, of the predictor variable (e.g., freeing children for adoption, as in Maas and Engler [1959]; focusing case planning on return home, as embodied in the Act of 1980; encouraging parents to visit; time spent in care). Nonetheless, there is no reason to believe that any goal can be achieved simply by re-creating the predictor variable through policy changes, concrete services, or counseling. Correlation is not cause and Finch, Fanshel, and Grundy (1986) need not squirm so with their observation that ser-

8. There is considerable controversy over this point. For example, Benedict, White, and Stallings (1987) and McMurtry and Lie (1992) report similar durations for black and white children, whereas many others such as Barth et al. (1994) report substantial differences. Also see the discussion in Courtney et al. (1996) and Mech (1983) on placement rates by race.

vices predict enduring care, that is, dependency may not be created by the services themselves. Instead, both services and long-term care are probably the result of the children's great needs.

The most sophisticated current research tends to endorse the pedigreed argument that structural factors, notably poverty, are the basic causes of the sudden and continuing growth of the child welfare system since the late 1980s. On the basis of an analysis of New York City administrative data, Wulczyn (1994) argues that there is a strong "connection between child placement and poverty" (181):

> The high rate of infant placement found in [New York City's] impoverished neighborhoods draws foster care closer and closer to the debate over poverty's coercive influence on family structure. While child welfare experts have always believed that poverty and foster care placement are intertwined, the epidemiological data needed to establish such relationships have never been available widely. (149)

Wulczyn presents strong epidemiological relationships between poverty and placement by way of choreographing steps "to unify family preservation services with health care." He claims that these services will minimize placements by addressing some of the structural deficits associated with poverty, namely, prenatal care, nutrition, and supportive community services. Others have made similar arguments to reduce poverty and, by extension, to preserve families (notably Lindsey 1994 and Pelton 1989). Lindsey proposes child welfare savings accounts and Pelton endorses the modest provision of concrete services (homemaker, respite, day care, housing, and income supports, to name a few) to reduce the influences of poverty on family dissolution. Still, the research is unable to trace changes in placements as a function of changes in poverty itself, a notably difficult methodological problem.

In the absence of any compelling and immediate proof of structural causation, the theme continually recurs that changes in the caseload are mediated either by administrative preferences (e.g., stiffer reunification criteria) or by deteriorating styles of living (e.g., drug use, crime, violence, marital discord) rather than by underlying social conditions beyond the control of the individual. Barth et al. (1994) emphasize the role of drugs and out-of-wedlock births in accounting for the recent increases in caseload in California, important by itself for containing approximately one-fifth of the nation's foster children. They analyze the different pathways of care, assuming that placement decisions can have important consequences for the child's outcomes. However, they count only the outcomes of legislated concern related to permanency—reunification, adoption, long-term care, and so forth. Yet their recommendations for improving outcomes, appended clearly to the end of each chapter in simplified tabular form, flow out of their claim to be able to identify "which elements of service are best for children's optimal growth and development" (21). However, this claim for differential treatment is not sustained even by their own research, which generally reflects the contemporary ignorance of child welfare services.

In the end, Barth et al. (1994) fail to provide more than a retrospective description of the dynamics of care in California—the length of time that children spend in different settings and the recorded reasons for the movement among them—based on questionably reliable administrative data.[9] Taken together with the more serious failure to measure either the children's actual outcomes or the quality of the settings, their research provides no authority for their recommendations.[10]

Their recommendations are focused on increasing permanent outcomes but they are uninformed about the desirability of the choices. Indeed, although their initial analysis points toward underlying social conditions as predicting the long-term child welfare caseload, their recommendations tinker with superficial services and questionably effective administrative changes. It would seem from their structural perspective that resolving drug abuse in natural parents and preventing unwise, single-parent births should be at the heart of any strategy to handle the foster care caseload. Yet there has been no demonstration of any ability to rehabilitate natural parents, to prevent family breakup, to prevent births among unmarried women, or to resolve other problematic behaviors such as substance abuse that are associated with child welfare placement.

The recommendations are best interpreted as a professionally convenient answer to a serious political problem. Permanency planning for the child welfare caseload seems to have failed but expensive alternatives are not politically viable. Barth et al. (1994) and the authors contributing to

9. The recent methodological enchantment with event-history analysis may be professional one-upmanship more than profound analysis. There is no assurance that the retrospective events are necessarily causative in the sense that changing them will change long-term outcomes. To the contrary, the placement events may simply be adaptations to current service constraints; they will appear to change as those constraints change. But in any event, the actual quality of care for the child may deteriorate or stay the same. Children's needs should be assessed through reliable procedures; statistical manipulation is a poor substitute for methodological rigor.

10. The same problems beset Courtney's (1994b) retrospective analysis of foster children in California, although he is clearer in concluding that "this study cannot establish whether [its] pattern of effects is 'good' or 'bad' for children placed in foster care" (104). Compared with other states, Courtney also found longer lengths of stay for foster care in California and that "in the first six months of 1988, more than 40 percent of all entering children remained in care for over 3 years" (99). Still, he handled censoring differently than many of his comparison studies.

Barth, Berrick, and Gilbert (1994) take the most frequent road to political fealty by retrieving permanency as a viable option: maintain budgets and manage the problem with small shifts in administrative emphases and re-designed services. Nevertheless, these conclusions do not flow out of the research but only out of the field's "practice wisdom," a contrivance of professionalism with even less empirical authority than Barth et al.'s (1994) pathways analysis.

Following an administrative logic, a variety of analysts have implicated placement decisions or other management practices in creating the large caseload. Goerge (1994) suggests that worker turnover has the unexpected effect of increasing discharges from foster care. He attributes this counterintuitive finding to the attention given to old cases by new workers. In doing so, he also draws attention back to the possibility that administrative changes in the system—more frequent case reviews—would likely have important impacts on caseload. Yet without actually evaluating the effects on children in care, it is impossible to assess whether the discharges are judicious consequences of prudent reviews. Instead, precipitous, unwise discharges might well result from administrative pressures on newly assigned caseworkers or from the increased likelihood that high staff turnover will eventually produce a caseworker with a greater tolerance for the perils of family reunification.

It should be no surprise that new agency goals imposed by administrative fiat would enjoy a measure of success at least in the short run. Employees tend to follow administrative directives. However, in the long run, forcing more children to return to their parents may produce tragedies. Indeed, much of the reported success of experiments in child welfare, discussed in the next chapter, may well have been due simply to staff compliance with administrative directives during the demonstration period and not to any enduring benefit. It is worth recalling that the reality of care for the child is infrequently assessed in any evaluation of services.

Children in group care seem to remain in the system longer than those in family foster care. Group care is also very expensive, often costing more than sixty thousand dollars per year for each child. Courtney (1994a) argues that preventing entrance into group care will tend to shorten a child's stay in the system generally. On the basis of an analysis of administrative data in California, he concludes that the initial placement decision itself—entry into a youth shelter—strongly predicts later use of group care. Therefore, he recommends "that it may be wise to increase efforts to avoid shelter care placement whenever possible" (201). If this is to be understood as more than a truism (it is good to be good), then the research is obliged to evaluate the needs and outcomes of the children themselves and not simply correlate entries to shelters with entries to group care. After all, the increasing prevalence of shelter care preceding group care would seem to be reasonable in light of the often repeated finding that children coming into care since 1985 seem to have more severe emotional and physical problems than earlier cohorts. Without identifying the independent contribution of the shelter placement itself, its selection as a cause of future placements appears to be arbitrary. The arbitrary decision to ascribe causal status to variables in a correlational analysis is a common failure of research.

Albert (1994) finds that a variety of factors—drug arrests, the number of births, the size of the welfare caseload, and the number of female-headed households—strongly predict changes in the foster care population. She therefore goes on to suggest a variety of targeted case service strategies to lower the number of unwanted births, reduce drug dependency, and assist poor female-headed families. However, the factors that Albert associates with foster care placement may simply mediate the true sustaining determinants of family failure with the result that her case service strategies may well be unsuccessful.

Indeed, all of the attempts to establish the effectiveness of family preservation, drug rehabilitation, prevention of repeat pregnancies, and family reunification, to name a few, have failed. There is little evidence, if any, to suggest that a series of superficial and poorly funded concrete services will have much success in lowering child welfare placements. For example, the addictive consequences of demon rum may be implicated in family dissolution. However, ending alcohol and drug dependency, a difficult if not impossible task, may have little effect on a deeply rooted psychological compulsion to escape a suffocating reality or an inability to control violent impulses that may be the true causes of family dissolution. Many failed parents may be beyond the curative powers of any structural or personal intervention. In a similar manner, many sins may be embedded in modern culture and without returning to the happier time of a world we have lost they will remain unpreventable and virulent.

In the end, Barth and Berry take considerable pride in the declining lengths of stay in foster care, attributing the change to the Act of 1980 (Barth and Berry 1994:329). However, the literature does not credibly substantiate any decline. The earlier studies they cite (e.g., Fanshel and Shinn 1978; Maas and Engler 1959) provided inflated estimates of duration in care while Barth and Berry ignore contradictory evidence (e.g., Jenkins 1967).[11]

Tatara (1993) reports that between 1977 and 1989 the median length

11. Nevertheless, Jenkins (1967) is not far different from Tatara (1994) or even Courtney (1994b). The lower estimates of length of care are based on unrestricted samples; the higher estimates are based on samples that ignored those in care fewer than ninety days. See also the next note.

of time in foster care declined from 2.4 years to 1.4 years. Yet these estimates are based on only 60 percent of the children in foster care. Moreover, the lengths of utilization are computed only from a one-day census
and do not capture the experience of the much larger number of children
who have left the system. In addition, the lengths of care are computed for
only a single episode of care and therefore neglect the lifetime utilization
of the child welfare system. This is a particularly large problem in light of
the many disruptions of adoptions and reunifications.[12]

Most important, however, the literature has not measured the effects on the
children of the possibly declining lengths of care. Indeed, even marginally
declining lengths of stay, let alone Tatara's large decreases, could well be
taken as evidence of an HMO effect (reduced care as a function of changed
incentives rather than declining need). Together with the increasing caseload and the declining number of available foster parents, the pressures
released by the Act of 1980 may have actually encouraged both premature
reunification and delayed placement. Yet Barth and Berry, two sophisticated researchers, choose to ignore both the limitations and contradictions
in earlier research to arrive at the professionally congratulatory conclusion
that progress has been made through informed policy development, that is,
permanency planning.

Although the duration research provides little if any basis to endorse
permanency planning (or any other of the nation's past enthusiasms for
care), it does forever stoke the flames of hope that marginal changes in
poorly funded social services will resolve the enduring problems of child
welfare. Hopeful leads constantly emerge out of the plausible but untested
predictor variables of correlational analyses. They become mythic diver-

12. The mischaracterization creates a "hospital bed" problem in which current utilization represented in the one-day census exaggerates lengths of care, failing to provide a true
picture of those utilizing care over a period of time. On the other hand, reporting only single
episodes of care understates lifetime utilization. Therefore, an accurate utilization picture requires a much wider time window, five years and perhaps much longer, during which the
lengths of stay of all who utilize the system are computed for both single episodes and lifetime utilization with adjustments for right-hand and left-hand censoring. The time window
needs to be aged to obtain estimates of changes. This has still not been done for any large
group of children in foster care. In short, Tatara reports average lengths of stay for *many who
are in care* instead of average lengths of stay for *all those who utilize the system* while ignoring
lifetime utilization. His mischaracterization results from the many inadequacies of the data
in the Voluntary Cooperative Information System. In turn, its imperfections probably reflect
longstanding inattention to child welfare services, an inattention that reflects the status of dependent children in American society. The data problems may be resolved with current plans
for a systematic child welfare reporting system. Yet with the devolution of federal authority
to the states, it is still quite likely that they will continue.

sions from the stark possibilities that services are inadequate for the many children in long-term care who have nowhere else to go and that the greatest number of misplacements are made in unwisely reunifying children with incompetent parents.

Duration in care and its narrow implications for utilization may be the real red herrings of child welfare. The central issue remains the quality of services for the children—their needs and their outcomes in care. Unfortunately, this is probably the most poorly researched area of child welfare services.

The Quality of the Child Welfare System

The ability of the child welfare system to respond to children's needs depends on the quality of its services. In turn, quality is measured by the capacity of the system to handle those needs, the outcomes of its separate services, and the degree to which care conforms with commonly accepted cultural values, starting with safety. Except for capacity itself—a simple count—the dimensions of quality defy easy measurement.

Decades of literature have produced very few and very poor estimates of the system's outcomes except in the most politically sterile notions of placement decisions themselves. For years, even this was uncertain. Moreover, the sufficiency or insufficiency of the system is a curious result not so much of objective capacity but of the society's definition of what constitutes need in the first place. Thus the discovery of frequent child maltreatment at the end of the 1960s increased the standard of need against which to evaluate the child welfare system.

In an important sense, the quality of child welfare services must be measured against equality and decency—the question of whether placements are homelike—and a sense of what the United States owes its children. Of course, there is always an implicit promise in child welfare services that investments in children will pay off in adults. However, the deeper meaning of child welfare services sets the minimum level of protection, maintenance, and enrichment that the United States defines as a right of citizenship even for its most vulnerable citizens.

Characteristics of Children in Care

Beyond the physical absence of parents or the presence of inadequate parents, the children who come into care are apparently very needy. Moreover, those who are placed in group care (also frequently called residential care, residential treatment, group foster care, and others) are needier than those in family foster care. However, only the rare study (e.g., Fanshel and Shinn 1978) has measured the needs of these children independently of the child welfare system itself (its personnel and its records). Most studies of children in care rely on notoriously unreliable administrative records while the state of the art of measuring children's conditions is seriously deficient: "As yet, we have no precise ways to measure emotional disturbance, developmental deficit, degree of family disorganization, treatment needed, or treatment received. What is available is professional judgment about such issues" (Frank 1980:257).

Relying on the scaled judgments of foster parents in Tennessee, McIntyre and Keesler (1986) found that about half of foster care children "manifested evidence of psychological disorder" (302). This finding of great psychological need has been widely corroborated in a variety of studies (e.g., Haynes et al. 1983; Hochstadt et al. 1987; Kirst and Wald 1989; Reid, Kagan, and Schlossberg 1988). Reporting on a subsample of Fanshel and Shinn (1978), Frank (1980) concludes that long-term foster care children have "severe psychological disturbance" and are receiving inadequate care (260). Moreover, Frank's subsample appeared to be more psychologically debilitated than reported by the agencies serving the children. Children with multiple placements apparently exhibit even greater behavioral problems (Fanshel, Finch, and Grundy 1989). Klee and Halfon (1987) conclude that foster children in California have a great amount of need for mental health services but that their needs are routinely ignored, a finding that is more generally supported (Hulsey and White 1989; Joint Commission on Mental Health of Children 1973; Maza 1983; Swire and Kavaler 1979; Wadsworth 1984).

Measures of other needs are equally troubling. Children in foster care are likely to adjust poorly to school (Canning 1974; Dumaret 1985). They are likely to exhibit more delinquency than the general population (Rogers and Leunes 1979). The problems of foster children apparently carry over into adulthood (Rest and Watson 1984). These differences between foster children and the general population have existed for at least forty years (McCord 1983).

The health of foster children is also troubling. In comparing a sample of foster children in Baltimore with the general pediatric population, Schor (1982) observes

> that children who have been under the protective and, hopefully, remedial care of the foster care system continue to demonstrate evidence of inadequate health supervision. Inadequate recognition and correction of refractive errors, incomplete immunizations, and the large number of unrecognized chronic problems all suggest that the medical care of foster children is not sufficiently frequent or comprehensive. (526)

Children in group care are needier than children in family foster care, evidencing a great number of behavioral and psychological problems. They have used many more prior services (Fitzharris 1985; Small, Kennedy, and

Bender 1991; Wells 1993; Wells and Whittington 1993). Commenting on children in group care in California, Berrick, Courtney, and Barth (1993) observe that "many show signs of acting out, aggression, sexual promiscuity, and substance abuse. Children served in specialized foster care are also seriously disturbed" (461).

Although no study appears to provide a comprehensive and independent assessment of the needs of foster children, the consensus of a variety of partial, regional, and otherwise limited research is that foster children, and particularly those in group care, have many unmet and serious problems apart from their obvious need for adult supervision. The absence of accurate and thorough information about their needs is itself an indication of the child welfare system's inadequacies.

Characteristics of Placements, Foster Parents, and Birth Parents

Basing its conclusions on the opinions of knowledgeable informants and a review of the literature, the U.S. General Accounting Office (GAO) documented a severe shortage of foster parents:

> Nearly every state is experiencing a serious shortage of foster families. In some states the shortage is so great that children are being shuttled from one place to another, such as temporary homes, institutions, or hospitals, until a proper home is found. There are reports that children, even preschool children, are being placed in child care institutions because appropriate foster homes are not available. Some children are sent to shelters or back to their birth home where problems may get worse. (GAO 1989:13)

Writing as early as 1973, the Joint Commission on Mental Health of Children concluded that

> foster parents are typically volunteers whose motives for engaging in such care are sometimes dubious, or they are the product of exhaustive and exhausting recruitment on the part of determined caseworkers attached to various placement agencies. Occasionally, families have been literally dragooned into accepting such a role. In any case, there are always too few of them, so that many homes are allowed to continue as foster placements even when there is a real cause to doubt the desirability of this practice in that particular setting. What it boils down to is that some home is so much better than no home that the situation continues. (277)

The situation has probably been growing worse since the reports from the GAO and the Joint Commission. The factors producing greater child need and a smaller supply of foster homes have all either intensified or remained prevalent: more children in care, declining incomes for working families at lower socioeconomic levels, high divorce and separation rates, and an enormous and growing number of two-worker families (Hernandez

1993). It is also worth speculating that an increasingly restrictive national policy has encumbered potential foster families with a greater economic burden to maintain themselves at the same time that it encourages unsuitable adults to become foster parents largely for economic reasons. Moreover, care for foster children may deteriorate during tougher economic times because "state reimbursement rates are generally too low to cover all the costs foster parents [should] incur in caring for children" (GAO 1989:15). Tough economic times themselves may create a supply of "volunteers," who seek out foster care as if it were a public works project. Indeed, it might be wise to restrict placements to more affluent families that will not draw on the reimbursements for their own needs. However, the American middle class, composed largely of two-worker families, provides relatively few foster parents.

As many have observed (Costin, Karger, and Stoesz 1996; Lindsey 1994), child welfare service moneys have been diverted both toward the investigation of complaints and protective services and away from longer term needs including foster parent recruitment and training. However, recruitment itself may be a dead-end strategy. Cultural attitudes, evidenced in part by popular enthusiasm for the welfare reform provisions of 1996 and other planks in three decades of conservative national policy, have tilted away from the care of children and become hardened against the poor. Moreover, the general quality of foster parents, notwithstanding an early claim of an abundant and highly skilled supply (Theis 1924), may have been marginal for decades, suggesting that current patterns of recruitment may be exhausting the potential for desirable foster parents.

The GAO (1989) focused on recruitment as an answer to the shortage of qualified foster parents. However, their respondents also implied that foster care would benefit from a variety of other relatively inexpensive program supports: foster parent training, more caseworkers, foster parent respite, greater private sector resources, information exchange, and even higher reimbursements. Yet there is little demonstration that any of these strategies provides more effective family foster care.[13]

Foster parents are typically middle-aged, blue-collar or semiskilled workers, with some high school education, who still have natural children living with them (Babcock 1965a, b; Fanshel and Shinn 1978; Fein, Maluccio, and Kluger 1990). Lindhom and Touliatos (1978) report that the mean age of foster parents is about forty and that they are predominantly lower middle class with an annual family income of $12,000 (the poverty line for a family of four in 1980 was $8,414).

Presumably the foster parents that Fanshel and Shinn (1978) assessed

13. Two of GAO's recommended training programs for foster parents, NOVA and MAPP, are discussed in the next chapter.

were among the more successful since they were able to maintain at least one foster child in their homes for more than three years. As a result, only about 5 percent of these foster parents were rated as performing their duties poorly. However, the small number of children in care for more than two years and the fact that all of the respondents to this portion of Fanshel and Shinn's study had provided very stable placements severely circumscribes the applicability of this finding to foster parents generally. More recent studies suggest a considerable problem with the quality of foster parents and foster placements.

It is hard to avoid the conclusion that many foster parents are motivated by foster care payments, inadequate as they may be—maximum board payments across the states averaged only $407 per month in 1994. Moreover, many foster parents are apparently too unskilled and poorly motivated to offer nurturing relationships; maltreatment may even be routine, occurring in 25 percent of foster homes (Zuravin, Benedict, and Somerfield 1997).

Fein, Maluccio, and Kluger (1990) studied all of the 779 foster children in Connecticut who had been in family foster care more than two years as of January 1, 1985. Similar to Fanshel and Shinn (1978), their sample tended to contain the more successful foster parents and probably even the more successful children, that is, children who seem to have adapted well to family care. They report that two-thirds of these foster parents were married, and foster families typically contained 3.3 children: 1.8 foster children, 0.4 adopted children, and 1.1 biological children. Averaging more than five people, 39 percent of these families earned less than $15,000 per year; 53 percent earned less than $20,000. (In 1985, the poverty threshold for a family of four was about $11,000 and a family of five, about $13,000, while Connecticut's median family income has been the highest in the nation for many years.) Single foster mothers comprised about one-third of the foster parent homes and fully 47 percent of them had incomes under $10,000 per year. In addition, they differed from married foster mothers in expected ways: lower educational attainment and probably a greater number of personal problems. An even larger proportion of single African American foster parents had incomes below the poverty line, confirming earlier research (Downs 1986). While reporting educational levels that were slightly higher than previous studies, only one-third of the foster parents had at least one year of college; married foster parents tended to have more formal education than unmarried foster parents. "Working and blue-collar occupations were prevalent" (40). As the authors note, foster parenting should be considered a "calling." However, it would take monumental ideological leaps to conclude that these foster parents were motivated by epiphanies of social responsibility rather than by more mundane financial considerations.

Rowe (1976), as well as a descendent literature that the GAO (1989) report relied upon, attempts to identify the determinants of successful foster parenting. Unfortunately, none of these studies evaluates foster care by distributing any of their criteria of successful foster parenting across even a sample of foster parents. That is, the research fails to document the extent to which a problem of fostering exists based on attitudes, social class, or other characteristics. Except for rare exceptions, the studies develop their criteria of success on a priori grounds, failing to actually relate foster parent characteristics to actual foster care outcomes. Rowe simply relies on the subjectivity of social workers to rate the success of foster homes. Rowe concluded that acceptance and tolerance of the foster child by the foster parent predicted successful parenting, although the predictions are quite weak. Yet even this weak finding is suspect since response rates to Rowe's questionnaire were low and probably produced, as he acknowledges, a biased respondent pool.

Although Fanshel and Shinn (1978) also relied on subjective measures of foster parenting, they provide a unique study of the relationship between foster parent characteristics and independently measured outcomes. They found that the intellectual climate of the foster home provided a substantial predictor of behavioral change in the child. Their findings suggested a customarily bleak setting for foster family care, especially in light of the relatively low level of educational attainment and employment among many foster parents and routine reports both of abusive foster family placements and placement disruptions. In spite of the field's concern with "bounce," few researchers attended to the deficiencies of the foster parents themselves in explaining placement failures.

Although weak, marginal, and perhaps even lacking the emotional and spiritual savoir faire to provide adequate parental guidance, foster parents still appear to be better custodians of children than the natural parents of the children in care. They also appear to be better educated and wealthier. On the basis of limited demographic information,[14] much has been made of the economic poverty of natural parents in order to argue that the absence of resources in the family has been the overriding if not the sole consideration in removing children.[15] This observation has also become one of the standard proofs for the structural perspective at the heart of the literature.[16] Much less credence is given to the compelling personal problems

14. Limited in the sense of providing inadequate information to characterize the other personal deficiencies of natural parents or to attribute the causes of their impoverishment.

15. In particular see Barth, Berrick, and Gilbert (1994); Berrick, Barth, and Gilbert (1997); Lindsey (1994); Pelton (1989); and Schuerman, Rzepnicki, and Littell (1994).

16. A perspective shared by Fein, Maluccio, Barth, Berrick, Gilbert, Costin, Stoesz, Karger, Lindsey, and the overwhelming proportion of child welfare researchers. Gruber (1978) among a very few others refuses to draw structural conclusions from his data or to

of parents, notably drug and alcohol addiction, emotional deficits, psychiatric impairments, and other behavioral aberrations that impede adequate parenting and that are probably also associated with if not actually causative of their poverty.

Numerous studies of foster care, frequently relying on administrative records and unsystematic worker opinions, report the many problems of birth parents. However, few studies provide independent substantiation of the presence or severity of these problems. Yet structuralists make the facile assumption that a simple array of concrete services will succeed in overcoming the maltreatment by birth parents and transform them into caring adults.

The literature abounds with descriptions of standards for parents and adequate care, such as Daly and Dowd's (1992) definition of a "harm-free, effective environment [for children in out-of-home care] as one that is not only free from abuse and neglect and in compliance with legal and licensing guidelines, but also promotes children's rights and offers children the opportunity to receive care and treatment that promote spiritual, emotional, intellectual, and physical growth" (489). However, the literature fails to apply these standards to either the natural or foster homes of the children in order to evaluate their actual situations.

The investigation of initial complaints of maltreatment, documentation of the use of services including drug and alcohol programs, opinions of the social worker, and so forth, are all flawed estimates of need among birth parents and obviously inadequate substitutes for objective information. In contrast, measures of income are relatively hard and natural parents appear to be a very impoverished group (among many others see Vasaly 1976). In this way, soft, easily questioned measures of parental disability alongside more reliable data about their economic plight have produced considerable confusion surrounding the issue of appropriate removal; children appear to be removed largely because their parents are poor and not because the parents are greatly incapacitated or because their maltreatment is chronic. The postmodern decree that the subjective judgments by social workers, among others, concerning the conditions of birth parents are conveying socially constructed preferences does not by itself undermine those judgments. Imperfect information on all sides creates a serious balancing problem among the interests of the child for protection, of the parents for authority over their children, and of the society for social cohesion, productivity, and justice.[17]

---

make structural assumptions, although the reason for his failure do so is even more illogical than the causal flaw in the structural position; see below.

17. With equal probity, the critical mood might easily focus on the postmodern ideological transgressions of the critic.

Pelton (1989) may be accurate in observing that "there is now over-whelming evidence of a strong relationship between poverty and abuse and neglect" (38). However, he ignores cultural poverty as a determinant of maltreatment, and his argument is marred by the many methodological problems of his sources, notably sample representativeness and unreliable data collection, in comparing these behaviors across socioeconomic groups.[18] Moreover, many of Pelton's sources (in both 1994 and 1989) are political bulletins, not serious empirical estimates of social conditions. Lindsey (1994) expands the base of support for Pelton's contentions. Still, nothing in the methodologies of these studies or of any other research confirms the causal relationship of economic poverty per se to maltreatment.

Nevertheless, it does appear to be accurate that the child welfare system draws principally from the poor, and as Pelton (1989) insists, the poorest of the poor (also corroborated by Lindsey 1994 and the authors in Barth, Berrick, and Gilbert 1994 and Berrick, Barth, and Gilbert 1997). At the same time, however, parents who mistreat their children appear to be less competent than a variety of comparison groups, including those of the poor on AFDC, reported in five weak, regional, small-sample studies (Gaudin and Dubowitz 1997). In addition, a variety of studies have documented the medical, mental, and emotional deficits of the birth parents whose children are placed. Yet again the relationship between economic poverty and parental incapacity is still empirically unproven.

Charges of inappropriate removal from birth parents—conjuring up a Nurse Ratchet insensitivity and a cultural imperialism oppressing the colorful, Left Bank, iconoclastic lifestyles of economically frayed but still caring parents—are substantiated to the degree that the quality of current foster parents becomes an acceptable standard of care. In this case, the placement choice is restricted to either inadequate natural parents or inadequate (although somewhat less so) foster parents. This choice, abetted by budgetary restraint, tends to weigh against removal. Yet the documentation for inappropriate removal as well as the capriciousness of child welfare decision making generally (see below) is not convincing; these studies implicitly use very sorry standards that accept the low quality of foster parents as inevitable for public services. In this way, the cultural intolerance of the worker slyly replaces parental deficiency as the cause of removal, creating the appearance of a great number of inappropriate decisions.

Curiously, the conclusion of inappropriate removal actually relies on the literature's inability to establish any fact convincingly but still holds to

18. The literature that Pelton cites in his 1989 book (e.g., Gil 1970; Kaplun and Reich 1976; Pelton 1981; U.S. Department of Health and Human Services 1981; Weston 1974; Wolock and Horowitz 1979) also ignores the problems of cultural poverty and commits many of his errors of interpretation.

a more general position that poverty itself is the cause of child maltreatment and placement. However, without near infinite knowledge, a residual logic is very chancy. Pelton (1989) argues that because the inadequacies of parents to provide appropriate care for their children have not been well established, economic poverty, which he can establish with some authority, is all that remains to explain both their deficiencies and removal. In this case, poverty is not an intractable cultural problem requiring that children be removed from their parents. Instead with supportive, concrete services, placements can be prevented and children can be successfully reunited with their parents. These services include emergency caretakers and homemakers, housing assistance, emergency cash assistance, accident prevention (rodent control, lead paint programs, and so forth), babysitting, day care and night care, parenting skills education, visiting nurses, parent aids, self-help support groups, substance abuse and other referrals to other health and welfare agencies, respite care, crisis intervention, and counseling, (Pelton 1989:163).

There is little recognition, however, that these services have failed to achieve their goals. Yet even if the full battery of services were to be provided at truly intensive levels, and this has never been tried, their very intensity would acknowledge a profound incapacity to parent children and therefore would argue forcefully for removal and not the perpetuation of abuse and neglect behind a trellis of supportive services. Essential emotional and social bonds with children have in all likelihood been broken and probably irreparably when parents require such an extensive array of support. It is notable that Pelton (1989) avoids any estimate of the extent to which his catalogue of care will succeed in preventing placement. The simple observation that children in foster care are drawn from among the poorest of the poor does *not* lead to the conclusion that repairing their material deficits will naturally lead to socially capable behavior. Furthermore, the therapeutic services that Pelton sneaks into his list of concrete care — counseling, drug and alcohol programs, and his allusion to referrals — have never credibly achieved their therapeutic goals.

In spite of its growing popularity, kinship care does not seem to be an improvement over non-relative care. Based on a very limited amount of information, kinship caregivers seem to be poorer, older, and less prepared to provide care than foster parents generally. Thornton (1987, 1991) characterizes kinship caregivers as typically older African American women who are struggling financially. Dubowitz, Feigelman, and Zuravin (1993), studying kinship care among a largely African American group of children in Baltimore, reported that almost 50 percent were placed with their grandmothers and about 30 percent with their aunts. The median age of caregivers was forty-eight years with 20 percent over the age of sixty. Almost

60 percent of the caregivers had not completed high school. The children typically entered households that already contained a median number of three children. Only one-third of the caregivers were married while more than 50 percent were not employed. The authors failed to obtain income information.

Barth et al.'s (1994) comparison of kinship caregivers with foster caregivers in California endorsed skepticism. Even while the response rate to their survey was only 14 percent, the authors still claim that their study "provided a depth of information that is not otherwise available" (201). Such as the survey was, kinship caregivers in comparison with foster parents are more often single (52% vs. 24%), less educated (26% vs. 10% without a high school diploma), more welfare dependent (33% vs. 6%), and far less wealthy ($32,000 vs. $52,000 total household income). It is notable that both groups reported more than 2.5 foster children per home and household income estimates include foster care payments that probably averaged about $400 per month in 1993. Thus approximately $12,000 per year, which was a substantial portion of reported incomes, was derived from state foster care payments.[19] If the assumption is made that nonrespondents were probably less well off than respondents, Barth et al. closely mirrors the bleak picture of kinship providers offered by others.

Some children in kinship care may benefit from a special family bond "with people who know them and their family background, traditions, and culture" (Barth et al. 1994:214). Still, the maintenance of responsibility for child care within the extended family may remain a problem for many foster children even while it resonates with American family myths (Dubowitz et al. 1994). Vulnerable African American children in kinship care, placed with aging relatives who are perhaps unable to provide adequate supervision, may be the unwitting victims of the romance of the autonomous African American community (e.g., Everett, Chipungu, and Leashore 1991).[20]

The conditions of group care are not systematically reported in the literature, except to note that the amount of residential care has not kept up with need even while the average facility has become much smaller

19. Kinship providers also reported spending $134 per month of their own money (about $4,000 per year on their 2.5 children) in addition to state payments on each child. This would have reduced their reported incomes by almost 25 percent, an amount so large as to cast additional doubt on an already highly defective survey.

20. Everett, Chipungu, and Leashore's (1991) position would be a bit more credible if any of their authors bothered to pursue systematic information about kinship care. Even the information that they provide, in particular chapter 9 by Leashore, McMurray, and Bailey, tends to indict their theme of the black community's autonomy. The project they report on, Volunteers for Children in Need, was able to reunite only eighteen out of sixty-two referred families. In spite of this paltry result, the authors congratulate themselves, suggesting a professional self-absorption that belittles the interests of children in need.

(Dore, Young, and Pappenfort 1984). It is impossible to discern the proportion of residential care for children that is deficient or the conditions of customary care. However, whatever its conditions, group care can be very expensive, frequently costing upwards of sixty thousand dollars per year for each child. Barth et al. (1994) surveyed group care facilities in California, finding high turnover within staffs that were relatively young and well educated. Other responses also varied greatly.[21]

While many foster care placements may at least stop abuse and provide a minimal amount of supervision, they also seem to be meted out in a fashion that denies middle-class comfort to children who by and large are drawn from lower socioeconomic levels. Foster care seems to have taken on the mission to maintain social class as part of its charge to address child maltreatment. The "less eligibility" of child welfare services may be a historical link if not actually an unacknowledged atavism to Elizabethan poor laws.

Quality of Placement Decisions

The wisdom of the decision either to remove children from their homes or to allow them to remain there is an essential component of evaluating the child welfare system. Particularly in light of the large proportion of child homicides that occur in families that are known to child protective agencies, a torrent of criticism has battered the system for unwisely leaving children in threatening situations. There has been considerable documentation of high recidivism back to foster care from reunified families and of disruptions in adoptions (Barth 1988; Barth and Berry 1988; Block and Libowitz 1983; Rzepnicki 1987; Wulczyn 1991). Moreover, Festinger (1996) estimates that recidivism, narrowly defined as return to care within two years of being discharged from care, reached almost 20 percent. Cautley and Aldridge (1973) and Fein and Maluccio (1984) reported that approximately one-third of foster family placements failed. Fein et al. (1983) reported that one-third of reunifications failed and that 50 percent of "permanent" foster care placements failed. Higher rates are routinely reported; counting all placement disruptions including foster care, Goerge (1990) estimates that as many as "60 percent of all children [in Illinois] who enter care experience unstable placement histories" (433). Adoption disruptions range from 6 percent to 20 percent and may be climbing (Barth and Berry 1994; Urban Systems Research and Engineering 1985). The high reentry rates to foster care and the great amount of adoption disruption suggest that a large proportion of permanency decisions, perhaps even taking place

21. As with their survey of kinship care, the authors only achieved a very low response rate (33%) on this survey.

with supportive social services, are ill-conceived and hasty. At the same time, the system is paradoxically viewed as inefficient, intolerant, and cruel for precipitously removing children from their parents and then inappropriately retaining them in care.

It is again notable that no study has independently assessed the children in care, their placements, and their home situation to determine the number of those in care who should not be there. By the same token, there is no study of the actual prevalence of child maltreatment in the population that would allow for precision in estimating the amount of unmet need for placement. As a consequence it is not clear that there is a decision-making problem except insofar as the increase in the number of children in care is irritating social tolerance.

Technically, the quality of decisions to remove and place maltreated children depends on the ability to assess at least the risks to the child. However, the more controversial problem is political: even with good knowledge of what is happening in the home, who should be removed, that is, how much risk is tolerable? Both the technical and the political problems require credible information.

Falling to a common temptation, Lindsey (1994) clearly acknowledges the poor quality of information in the field generally but then relies on it. In demonstrating the unreliability of the decision-making process, he cites three studies of social workers' attitudes in hypothetical situations (Briar 1963; Donnelly 1980; Phillips, Haring, and Shyne 1972) while pointing to their debilitating flaws.[22] Based on variable worker attitudes he concludes that "a limited consensus exists on what criteria should be used in removing a child from the homes" (135). He might also have pointed out that worker attitudes, especially those measured in research interviews, may have little effect on their actions in field situations in which their personal discretion is presumably limited.

After excusing his use of flawed information in his three cited studies as being "the best current indicator," Lindsey (1994) applies these estimates of unreliable decision making to one hundred hypothetical cases. He insists that the results confirm Pelton's "suspicion":

> There are certainly some children of those endangered by severe harm for whom placement in foster care, despite its known deficiencies and attendant harms, would be the relatively *least* detrimental alternative. But who are these children who cannot be protected in their own homes by less disruptive and relatively harmful means than child removal? It is my

22. In coming to the same conclusions Pelton (1989) relies on Besharov (1985); Mnookin (1973); Phillips, Shyne, and Haring (1971); and Wald (1976). At least Phillips et al. can be read very differently (see below).

belief that not only are there many children in foster care who should *not* have been placed there, but that there are other children who are being wrongfully *left in* their natural homes. In short, children are being removed from their homes in the *wrong* cases and being left at home in the *wrong* cases. Furthermore, it is my belief that if only those children were placed in foster care who would actually need it, we would have very *few* children in foster care. (emphasis in original; Pelton 1989:67)

Lindsey (1994) and many others tie possible placement errors—the caprice of removal—to the observation that foster children are drawn disproportionately from poor families, thereby underwriting a more general attack on the system for its animus toward the poor.

Children have been removed because the court disapproved of the parents' life style or child rearing practices. Removal has occurred, for example, because the parents were not married, because the mother frequented taverns or had male visitors overnight, because the parents adhered to extreme religious beliefs or lived in a communal setting, because the parent was a lesbian or male homosexual, because the parents' home was filthy or because the woman was the mother of an illegitimate child. In none of these cases was there evidence of harm to the children. In such instances, socially unacceptable behavior of the parents is condemned on the pretext of acting in the child's best interest. (Stein, Gambrill, and Wiltse 1978:5)

Pelton, at least, displays the virtue of acknowledging his conclusions as personal beliefs. However, the system's purported failures, in particular inappropriate removal, are more commonly awarded the cachet of credible social science but without credible research. Stein, Gambrill, and Wiltse (1978) cite only Wald's (1975) admittedly light and unrepresentative documentation in support of the conclusion that "in none of these cases was there evidence of harm to the child" prior to removal (5).[23] Wald based his conclusions on "a review of appellate cases" and he acknowledges that "appellate cases dealing with neglect are relatively rare, however, and may not be representative of normal court practices" (1033 n. 254). After all, Wald as well as the rest of the field are unable to measure the extent to which either current standards for removal or their own preferred standards are unmet. Yet they certainly intend this conclusion to be taken as generally applicable.

In contrast, Phillips, Shyne, and Haring 1971 can easily be read to endorse the reasonableness of the decision to remove children from their

---

23. This whole section and particularly this conclusion are actually Wald's words and not theirs (see Wald 1975:1033).

homes since the children who were placed, although poor, came from families

> that had exhausted their resources for help with their problems. Their mothers were more likely to have a history of mental illness, to appear emotionally disturbed, to have difficulty in holding a job and managing money, and to show a lack of concern for the children and inappropriate handling of them. If the father or a father figure was present in the home, he was much more likely in placement cases to evidence a range of deviant behavior and attitudes than the father in an own home service case. (Phillips, Shyne, and Haring 1971:86)

Knudsen (1988) also supports the consistency and appropriateness of judgments that substantiate maltreatment.

> Despite the high degree of discretion granted to child protective service workers, there is no evidence of a persistent systematic bias in the evaluation of this population of reported cases. The obvious conclusion—not refutable at present—is that the decisions were made on the basis of the degree of injury or danger to the child. (Knudsen 1988:154)

Still, the substantiation of maltreatment is not itself tantamount to removal, and the importance of Knudsen's retrospective analysis is also circumscribed by its location and data. Although it did cover the periods before and after the 1974 legislation that mandated the reporting of child maltreatment, the study was conducted in a relatively small metropolitan area in Indiana that does not appear to be similar to most urban centers in the United States. Moreover, the data were collected from administrative records that are customarily problematic in child welfare agencies. There was no independent verification of the accuracy of the information; this was of course impossible.

In short, the literature hardly provides consistent evidence of caprice, and a variety of studies (notably Hulsey and White [1989] and their cited lineage of supportive studies as well as Widom [1994]) have endorsed the probity of removal. Reasonable judges may differ, especially when many placement decisions appear to be difficult: the situation for the child is obviously bad but the ability of the parents to provide at least a minimal level of care is at issue. There is no reason to assume that in the absence of good risk assessment—and the system will surely continue to operate without a refined ability to forecast human behavior—ambiguous decisions are necessarily bad ones especially when errors occur on the side of the child's security and comfort.

Still, Lindsey expresses the field's orthodoxy in reaching confident conclusions that the decision-making process is culturally biased against poor people and that the bias results in many inappropriate removals. On the basis of his own research, Lindsey concludes that "unequivocally, the discriminant analysis indicated that children were being removed from their parents and placed in foster care *because* their parents possessed inadequate income security" (Lindsey 1994:141, 1991; emphasis added).[24]

It is noteworthy that Lindsey's 1994 book embellishes his 1991 finding that "those with government support were less likely to have their children removed than those with self-support wage income" (1991:274, 1994: 141). In 1994 he appends to this finding his conclusion that "clearly, government income support (i.e., welfare) prevents placement" (1994:141).

Unfortunately, this conclusion about cause and effect does not follow at all from his cross-sectional data. Indeed, simply increasing the income of people driven into poverty by behavior problems will not necessarily improve their behavior. Moreover, Lindsey (1992) seems to suggest a small relationship between financial and housing needs on the one hand and placement on the other; among Lindsey's predictors, these "environmental" reasons for seeking services and placement have the smallest odds ratio (0.28 as compared with "dependency" with a ratio of 2.21).

Lindsey (1994) for one is quite well aware of the analytic and interpretive problems that the weak literature present, even citing Gordon (1988:95): "Neither the social workers nor contemporary researchers studying the case records could easily distinguish children's deprivations caused by poverty from those caused by parental indifference and hostility: because parental indifference and hostility were among the most common products of poverty, and because parents' depression was implicated both as a cause and effect of poverty." Gordon might have also been a bit more forthcoming in acknowledging the methodological obstructions to test whether poverty causes indifference, hostility, and depression or in contrast whether they produce or even sustain poverty.

In the end, none of the studies offered by Lindsey, and certainly neither his discriminant analysis nor his hypothetical reasoning on the basis of very flawed research, actually support the conclusion that children are removed solely or even largely for reasons of poverty. The disproportionate number of children placed from "lone-parenthood" homes may have been removed from maltreating parents and not simply because of their poverty. Both the poverty of these single parents and the maltreatment of their children may reflect personal problems that are not amenable to any sort of quick and

24. Lindsey's book *The Welfare of Children* (1994) is certainly an impressive piece of scholarship. There is hardly another recent work that even attempts a sophisticated analytic clarity. Nonetheless, it is flawed by its commitment to a particular point of view, in this case structuralism, which underpins its polemical logic. Had it more clearly separated proofs of its tenets from their application, it could not have underwritten its final recommendations.

easy supportive or therapeutic care. And again, the issue of the causes of both the poverty of single parents and of parental misbehavior are still indeterminate. Indeed, there are numerous reasons—the underreporting of maltreatment and the intractability of many parental problems—to believe that far too few children are removed.

No conclusion about the quality of the placement decision can be sustained by the research. Yet the dominant voices in the literature proceed from uncertain information to firm conclusions. This curious rhetoric of picking over the tatters of research to stitch together a convenient cloth of social policy is tendentious not scientific, a tribute to the triumph of moral and political conviction over objectivity.

Outcomes of Foster Care

Obviously, the effect of foster care on foster children is the central element in evaluating its quality. However, a large number of ambiguous studies fail in the end either to measure the impact of foster care or to describe accurately the conditions of foster children who mature out of care. The studies typically lack controlled comparisons or their comparisons are misleading, or both. Few of the studies are able to describe accurately the social, emotional, health, or psychological characteristics of the children who enter care, while none of the studies adequately sample children even within their limited geographic areas. The samples of different studies are customarily not comparable. While it is apparent that many foster children are not doing well when they leave care, it is not apparent whether their deficiencies are due to the flaws of foster care or simply to the gravity of the problems that they bring to foster care. Even more profoundly, the expectations for behavioral change in children under a variety of environments are simply not known.

Barth (1990) made heroic attempts to contact recently emancipated foster children—a notoriously difficult group to either find or interview. Still, he succeeded in interviewing 75 percent of his identified sample of eighty-five former foster children in the San Francisco Bay area. At the time of the interviews the sample averaged twenty-one years of age. His sample may be less representative of all children who use the foster care system at any point in their lives and more representative of youths who enter care later and age out of the system. Acknowledging his "very accidental" sample, Barth claims that it probably contains more favored youths: the best prepared academically and those with good relationships with social workers and foster parents, and with homes at the time of the interviews. Even so, he found that only 55 percent had graduated from high school; only 53 percent rated their health as excellent or very good, with 38 percent reporting that they had untreated health problems and little financial access to care; 40 percent of the total sample (which was 53% female) reported a pregnancy since leaving foster care; the respondents had great difficulty with housing; 24 percent were involved in criminal activities since leaving foster care; many had "marginal attachments to the labor force; . . . many youth complained that they were allowed to just drift away without any services, guidance, pep talks, or good byes" (434).

> The low and high points of their lives since foster care or group care were queried. The nadirs were commonly associated with homelessness or financial hardship. The high points are modest at best and often involved finding companionship. . . . A striking 29% reported that there was a time [after leaving foster care] that they had no home or were moving about every week or more. (Barth 1990:430)

Under the auspices of a commission empaneled by the governor, Gruber (1978) conducted a one-day census of "every child in foster home care in Massachusetts," also obtaining data on a random sample of birth and foster parents. While the one-day census oversamples the long stayers, these children constitute the heart of the system's perceived problems. Only 27 percent of birth parents responded to the survey. About 70 percent of them had not graduated from high school, only 27 percent were still in their first marriage, and probably 70 percent had incomes under the poverty line. The fact that many poor people did not place their children was sufficient to convince Gruber that poverty played little role in family dissolution.

Gruber felt that the children's older age in comparison with earlier cohorts of foster children and the severity of their problems accounted for long stays in the system; he also identified a variety of administrative impediments to appropriate services. Perhaps reflecting the limitations of a one-day census, the foster parents appear to be more stable, more motivated, and a bit more financially comfortable than reported in other studies. Gruber's cautious conclusions pointed to the failures of foster care in Massachusetts to move children into permanent placements and to adequately handle the problems of its long-staying charges. He went on to recommend steps to prevent placements, increase the number of adoptions, and deliver services to children in care.

The study was published after the state failed to implement his recommendations, a failure that Gruber attributes to limited public interest and the short "issue life" of commission reports. It is notable that the study's cross-sectional limitations, among many others, prevented any estimate of the effects of the system itself on the children. Quality was simply assumed to be a feature of superficial conditions and lengths of stay.

As noted previously, many studies point to the great needs of children in foster care. However, the designs of these studies prevent attributing those needs to the failures of foster care itself in spite of the many suspicions that foster care routinely provides "inadequate homes" (Joint Commission 1973:69). Nevertheless, the research does document the emotional, educational, mental, physical, and behavioral deficits that the public child welfare system is at least formally mandated to address (Bohman and Sigvardsson 1990; Bryce and Ehlert 1971; Canning 1974; Frank 1980; Schor 82). However, the persistence of correctable deficits in at least physical health (Chernoff et al. 1994; Dubowitz et al. 1994; Halfon, Mendonca, and Berkowitz 1995; Risley-Curtiss et al. 1996) and mental health (Anderson and Simonitch 1981; Glisson 1996; Halfon, Berkowitz, and Klee 1992; McIntyre and Keesler 1986; Stein et al. 1996; Stein et al. 1994) suggest a more general concern with the quality of child welfare services and a pattern of public neglect even after the children are in care and their needs have been identified.

These bleak assessments of foster care's effects are contradicted by a variety of other studies that report either favorable outcomes of care or outcomes that are comparable to the general population. Yet none of these studies are credible. In perhaps the earliest systematic evaluation of the outcomes of foster care, Theis (1924) found that nearly 80 percent of foster children who were placed during the first twenty-five years of the New York State Charities Aid Association had grown into "capable" adults. However, this sample of foster children who had reached the age of eighteen may have had a special, unusual experience. "The Association made an effort to help every homeless child suitable for family life to find a foster home, but naturally the demand by foster parents for certain types of children determined to a large extent the group actually placed" (12). Moreover, Association workers themselves collected information and made judgments about "capability." Reliability was not checked. Yet this cohort of former foster children differed considerably from those then currently in care; they had come into care as older children, a far smaller percentage were adopted, and their foster homes were far more modest. Foster parents were apparently very difficult to recruit during the earlier years and only apparently well-adjusted, pleasant, easily disciplined children may have succeeded in being placed.

Nevertheless, positive evaluations of foster care have persisted to the present. Fein, Maluccio, and Kluger (1990) seem to show that children fare well in foster care. They measured the functioning of children in four areas: school, behavioral, emotional and developmental, and family adjustment. However, as in most other studies, they did not collect independent assessments of the children but relied on questionably accurate collateral judgments, in this case the foster parents'. As the authors report, "ease in disciplining the foster child was the best predictor of the child's functioning in all areas except family adjustment" (28–29). Perhaps anxieties over discipline colored all of the assessments by foster parents. Moreover, the sample contained only children living in foster family care for at least two years. Presumably the more difficult children had been screened into group care of one sort or another. Moreover, the authors fail to disaggregate their results or compare them with similar non–foster care children.

Fanshel and Shinn (1978) conducted a notable prospective study to evaluate the progress of children in foster care over five years. This longitudinal assessment is one of the very few studies that actually took independent and repeated assessments of their subjects in addition to the reports of collaterals. Unfortunately, they did not employ any control, and their sample was restricted to 624 children under thirteen years of age who had entered their first placement and who remained in care for more than ninety days. In the end, the authors were uncomfortable with their own findings that foster care is not particularly harmful:[25]

> We are not completely sure that continued tenure in foster care over extended periods is not in itself harmful to children. On the level at which we were able to measure the adjustment of the children we could find no such negative effect. However, we feel that our measures of adjustment are not without problems. (Fanshel and Shinn 1978:478)

However, they were only able to compare children who remained in foster care with those who had left. Their conclusions therefore cannot be usefully anchored either in reference to the general population of children outside the child welfare system or to a population of children that represent some more highly desirable level of functioning. It is even notable that the IQ scores of children who remained in care were enhanced during their first two and one-half years compared with those who went home. However, more than 50 percent of the total sample entered care performing below their age-appropriate level in school and still failed to achieve age-appropriate levels after five years in care. Indeed, without relevant comparisons, Fanshel and Shinn's findings defy easy interpretation, failing to establish (except perhaps in the case of school performance) the age-specific expectations for foster children. While they conclude that foster care does not do any *apparent* harm, which would also seem to be the conclusion of a parallel and supportive study (Fox and Arcuri 1980), it is also worth noting that it does not do any apparent good either, seeming to provide care that is perhaps superior only to maltreatment by abusive natural families. Contradicting their strong desire for permanency, foster

25. It is curious that Pelton (1989) as well as others occasionally cite Fanshel and Shinn (1978) and Shyne and Schroeder (1978) as "calling attention to serious faults in the foster care system" (Pelton 1989:53).

care emerges as frequently preferable to reunification, which, as reflected at least in IQ achievement, may renew abusive conditions.

Runyan and Gould conclude that "foster care placement of maltreated children does not appear to have a clearly detrimental effect on the child victims. Children in foster care are not at increased overall risk of juvenile delinquency when compared with peers left in home care" (1985:567). On the basis of a record search, the authors compared children in care with a matched group of children who were left in their own homes after a report of maltreatment. Yet, if criminal activity is to be investigated, then a more targeted study needs to be conducted since the expected amount of criminal activity while in care is relatively low; only ten children in the foster home group and eight children in home care committed crimes. Moreover, it appeared that foster care in this study of six North Carolina counties may have been as inadequate as the home life for the children; 25 percent of the matched children were subsequently maltreated by their parents while about 10 percent of the foster children were maltreated while in care. There were additional unconfirmed reports of abuse in both groups. The more appropriate conclusion may be that foster care in this community is no better than home conditions among maltreating families. This is not cause for celebrating family preservation but it is probable cause for indicting foster care.

Meier (1965) studied a small responding sample of former foster family children in Minnesota who had been in care at least five years. Only 95 out of 655 children who were in care during the time window of the study met its inclusion criteria. Meier found that her 75 respondents grew up to be "indistinguishable from their neighbors as self-supporting individuals; living in attractive homes; taking care of their children adequately, worrying about them, and making some mistakes in parenting; sharing in the activities of their neighborhood; and finding pleasure in their associations with others" (206). However, as Meier notes, they were in foster care during the Great Depression, suggesting serious economic considerations as the overriding cause for placement. In addition, the special conditions of Minnesota at that time—relatively rural and ethnically homogeneous—and the very small population that she sampled raise additional questions about the representativeness of her findings.[26]

Other studies suggest that the outcomes of foster care are desirable at least in comparison with abusing families or abusive situations (Kent 1976;

26. Conducted at a similar period of time although in Glasgow, Scotland, Ferguson (1966) concluded that "overall, their performance fell seriously short of that of the ordinary run of young people, not so much in employment record—though that presented disquieting features—as in social adaptation" (138).

Leitenberg et al. 1981; Palmer 1979). Again, all of these studies are seriously flawed methodologically. However, their most serious shortcoming is comparing the progress of foster children solely to standards that are themselves unacceptable, such as abusive parents and homes, while failing to compare the outcomes of foster care to standards or to groups that represent acceptable cultural norms (e.g., Dubowitz et al. 1994:102).

Festinger, a major apologist for foster care, concludes that those who leave foster care mirror the general experience of Americans: "Some fare a little better, some a little worse, but most are functioning in society in about the same ways as others their age" (1983:252). Yet she relied on very selective samples of former foster children and her study sustained nonresponse rates over 50 percent. Recognizing a problem does not solve it, or people would be immortal: "Of course, some will question the comparability of the two samples, and others will worry about those we never reached" (227). Nevertheless, the consistent deficiencies of former foster children that she does report—lags in education and emotional problems—suggest youthful deprivations that continue into adulthood. Finally, the success of some foster care children may be due to the strengths that they bring along with them into foster homes in spite of those situations. Festinger might answer her own question "Why do people tend to make dire predictions about those who have spent many years in foster care?" with her own comments about selective judgments. Her study is a gloss of foster care, relying on the recall of a highly screened group of respondents that appeared to be constituted with an eye to justify professional practice. However, it is not necessary to accept either the sanctity of the family or the desirability of public alternatives to embrace the discomforting conclusion that both seem to be routinely failing for many children.

In light of other equally impressionistic works that indict the quality of foster care (Gelles and Straus 1988; Toth 1997), the burden of proof would seem to lie with those who easily accept the current quality of care. This burden has not been credibly borne by Festinger (1983).

Cultural Optimism

More than seven decades of serious research in child welfare has still not produced credible descriptions of the public child welfare system. The body of the literature has barely graduated from anecdote. The most rudimentary data are lacking; only recently has there even been any accurate estimates of the number of children in care.

The researchers themselves seem unwilling to take a hard look at services. Money for evaluation, after all, flows largely from the public child welfare system itself. Private as well as public auspices are customarily blinded by cultural optimism, preferring to fund studies of hopeful leads rather than accurate estimates of what is commonly acknowledged to be a problematic system of care. The lack of credible research is an expression of an ineffective but socially efficient system of poor-quality care.

Unless genetics plays some unlikely but central role in determining the outcomes of foster children, it is perhaps reasonable to reach two tentative conclusions. First, prior to care, foster children lived in sorry circumstances that seem to have harmed their development; and second, foster care and the rest of the child welfare system have failed to repair those deficiencies. Even the studies that suggest the benign effects of foster care leave grave doubts about its quality. Perhaps to forestall an imagined hoard of poor but selfless parents from relinquishing their children to a generous system of care, public child welfare seems inspired by less eligibility, ensuring the meanest level of working-class life for its wards.

The findings that describe the system are amenable to ideological re-interpretation. In particular, the research expresses its biases most clearly as it attempts to ascribe causal status to structural variables. Yet its structural logic is paired with recommendations for only superficial and compatible interventions. This overarching commitment to social efficiency conforms with popular conservative tastes, explaining perhaps the drift of liberals to the right. It is understandable for professionals to guard their own interests however their self-protection obscures the inadequacies of public care, depriving the children of a just advocacy.

3
Experiments with Truth

The extensive but flawed body of descriptive research, reviewed in chapter 2, attempts to document the problems of public child welfare in the United States. These descriptive studies, frequently claiming to identify causal agents, have inspired social service interventions through the simplistic logic of paired conditions. The dominant, structural logic of the research argues that since poverty is associated with the growing child welfare caseload, concrete services need to be provided to families at risk to soften the effects of economic deficits and to reduce poverty itself. In contrast, the minority theme in the literature actually dominates politics: the behavioral imperfections and character deficits of parents explain child removal and family dissolution and therefore counseling and therapeutic services are needed to improve their moral quality.

Social experiments have been devised to test the effectiveness of a variety of these interventions—concrete and therapeutic—usually in reducing the public child welfare caseload, which is broadly accepted as the system's largest problem. Both as applied tests of theory and as estimates of social value, social experiments also shape scholarly inquiry. These experiments evaluate empirically the production functions of social services, that is, the experiments estimate the degree to which the social services actually achieve their stated goals. In this way, the experiments sanction social policy by commending the wisdom of one strategy or another. By extension, they inevitably influence the social dialectics and the political organizing that determine the outcomes of factional conflicts over scarce resources.

These two roles of research—neutral evaluation and policy guidance —are not naturally compatible, especially when the professional and political stakes in the outcomes of social services are considerable. Successful services imply a certain amount of social harmony. On the other hand, inadequate services and unmet needs impel a search for alternatives and therefore a reconsideration of social, political, and budgetary priorities.

The sociology of the social sciences—the social stakes in research and the way they are played out—is created by the political implications of research, particularly research that challenges authority.

The social experiments that test the effectiveness of child welfare interventions constitute the critical responsibility for the academic side of the human services. Taken broadly they also represent the promise of the social sciences to inform public policy. In turn, the outcome of the research bolsters one position or another, creating a constant temptation to exert influence in guiding inquiry toward agreeable conclusions. The lures and punishments of embedded orthodoxies—the expressions of power—prejudice the definition of the research problem (its narrowness or expansiveness), sampling design, analysis, and most obviously, the interpretation of findings. Researchers who devise compatible solutions to problems are revered; their careers are enhanced, their consultantships increased, and their future research funded. Researchers who contest the efficacy of established service orthodoxies tend to be ignored and their research proposals remain unfunded.

The appearance of success is frequently an adequate ceremonial substitute for success itself. Indeed, the experimental literature that underpins the current policies of the child welfare system—permanency planning, family reunification, family preservation, and their attendant social service interventions—is not scientifically credible. It fails to establish a rational authority for any conclusion, except perhaps the failure of the superficial interventions of current child welfare policy. Its errors are obvious and the drift of its conclusions conform to the socially efficient demands of contemporary politics.

Particularly in recent decades, the distortions of the child welfare literature are most often instances of an unmoored liberalism's conscious acquiescence with a popular conservatism in denial of social responsibility for the problems of many citizens. With only rare demurrals, the child welfare experiments leading up to the Act of 1980 and later studies have scripted one fantasy after another that superficial, inexpensive, and politically compatible social services can remedy deep cultural deprivations.

Experiments that Justified Permanency Planning and the Act of 1980

In one of the early efforts at family reunification, Sherman, Neuman, and Shyne (1973) attempted to address the most fashionable problem of child welfare of that time—children drifting in care. They designed a one-year demonstration to reunite parents with their children based on two elements. First, the demonstration implemented a monitoring system to ensure that children in care would be planned for and tracked. Second, special case-workers were trained "to work intensively with the natural parents" (7). The main features and criteria of the program were:

> The families selected for the project had to be recently known to the agency; the service given to them would be intensive and time-limited (clients seen on a weekly basis for 6 months); one or both natural parents had to be available for contact with the worker; the regular foster care workers would continue to provide service to the children and their foster families; and the special worker would continue supervision of the child in the natural parent homes after discharge from foster care. (Sherman, Neuman, and Shyne 1973:7)

Because of funding constraints the demonstration was conducted within only one large agency. The study was restricted to children in care "for whom return home seemed most likely" (Sherman, Neuman, and Shyne 1973:13). This focus translated into the selection for the experiment of 413 children who had been in care less than "3 years since their last separation from [their] natural or adoptive parents," who were under thirteen years of age, and who had at least one parent in the community whose parental rights had not been terminated (13). The children were then assigned (through a nonrandom process that the authors fail to specify) to one of three groups: a group that was monitored, a group whose natural or adoptive parents received intensive casework services from a "special worker," and a control group that received only the customary services of the agency.[1]

Two special workers were assigned to the intensive casework group. The special workers attempted to influence all of the cases in the group by serving as "in-house advocates" for reunification with the natural parents and by selecting cases that might benefit from their extra attention. Thirty-seven cases were selected by the special workers for intensive care.

> The special workers reported a full range of services provided to the clients [the thirty-seven cases] by the host agency or others, including financial assistance, medical service, etc., as well as services specifically initiated or arranged for by the special workers, including vocational training, legal service, group counseling, psychological testing and recreational service. (Sherman, Neuman, and Shyne 1973:43)

---

1. The children recruited during the first eight months of the project were disproportionately assigned to the control group and to the monitoring groups. As a result of non-random assignment and transfers during the experiment, the children in the special worker group had been in care longer than the other groups with perhaps uncontrolled consequences for reunification rates.

Whether comparing the controls with the full experimental group or with only the thirty-seven cases that received special, intensive casework, there were no differences in outcomes. Seven of the 37 special worker cases (19%) compared with 68 of the 376 control and monitoring cases (18%) returned to their parents. Only 13 percent of the 126 children in the total special worker group were returned to their parents, a lower percentage than in either of the other groups. There were no statistically significant differences between the control group and the monitoring group. Moreover, of the 75 reunifications across all three groups, 20 children (27%) returned to care. This recidivism was "evenly distributed over" the three study groups, however, the authors anxiously retrieve some value for their demonstration by pointing out that "none of the nine children whose discharges were arranged by the special workers were returned" to foster care. The authors offer a mix of "interpersonal, emotional, and environmental" factors that explain the failure of reunification.

The extra services provided to the experimental subjects—two additional workers for a caseload of 126—hardly constitute intensive care and therefore the lack of group differences is not surprising. It is unclear whether intensive casework in any form has ever been successful (discussed below).

The research design of Sherman, Neuman, and Shyne (1973)—particularly the absence of randomization and the use of questionably reliable measures—is obviously flawed, but its imperfections do not adequately explain the degree to which it is ignored in the literature. Few of the major current reviews of foster care even cite this study, although they all spend considerable time with the other experiments in permanency planning that were conducted in the 1970s. Compared with its contemporaries that encouraged passage of the Act of 1980, Sherman and colleagues' principal distinguishing characteristic is its negative findings and not its pliable methodology.

Burt and Balyeat (1977), following the recommendations of an earlier evaluation of the child protective system in Nashville, Tennessee (Burt and Blair 1971), tested the effectiveness of a newly designed comprehensive emergency services (CES) system. CES was designed to reduce the number of unjustified maltreatment petitions, precipitous child removals, inappropriate placements, and costs. In contrast with the system it replaced, CES offered a number of emergency services (caretaker, homemaker, foster homes, family shelters, and child shelters) as well as outreach and follow-up components and a redesigned juvenile court program. The results of this three-year demonstration in Nashville appeared to provide grounds for national recommendations that strongly influenced the Act of 1980.

The program's experience was evaluated by comparisons between the system that operated three years before the implementation of CES and the second year of CES's operation. These comparisons produced evidence of dramatic change. The number of filed petitions declined by 56 percent; the number of screened cases in which a petition was not filed increased by 180 percent. The number of removals decreased by 51 percent. The number of children placed in expensive residential care declined by 87 percent. The number of children under the age of six who were institutionalized declined from 180 to zero. The number of recidivist cases declined by 88 percent, representing a decline in the recidivism rate from 16 percent to 9 percent. The number of children with delinquency records declined from 44 to zero. Moreover, the new system in spite of its enhanced services cost less than the old system. On the basis of these findings the authors unfurled a banner of victory:

> In this time of increasing public concern over neglected and abused children, a program based on practical considerations and which has been demonstrated to be cost-effective should be publicized throughout the country. The success of the CES system has caused the [federal government] to establish in Nashville the National Center for Comprehensive Emergency Services for the express purpose of disseminating information about the system and encouraging its adoption in other states and communities. (Burt and Balyeat 1977:83)

Yet in spite of this newly funded, secular church of the practical and its mission to propagate a faith in CES, Burt and Balyeat's (1977) evaluation is seriously flawed as credible proof that the documented changes justify its conclusions and recommendations. In the instances in which the authors provide data on each of the five years covered, it is apparent that many of the outcomes had already been changing. Ignoring the project year 1970–71, the decline appears to be linear during each of the other years between 1969–70 and 1973–74 in the number of petitions filed and the number of families cited with maltreatment petitions. Without a true experimental design (the program neither randomized children to a control nor selected any similar community for comparison) it is not apparent that the program was more than associated with the changes it claims to have caused.

The evaluation took no direct measures of the situations of the children either before or during the experiment. All outcome measures were based on dispositions (remaining home, petitions filed, etc.). Thus the project cannot conclude in any sense that the children themselves were better off. As one example, the project measured the "*quality* of foster home placements" as the *number* of children who were placed "in same foster home, in another foster home, with relatives, returned home, and adopted" (Burt and Balyeat 1977:55). The assumption that returning children to their parents is invariably preferable to foster care takes a blind leap of faith in the absence of reliable assessments of the children's actual situations. CES's assurance that repeat maltreatment reports and other measures of recidivism picked up repeated maltreatment is highly suspect in light of family migration and the large amount of unreported maltreatment. Moreover, CES's desire to reduce the number of reports may have been subtly communicated to Nashville residents in a manner that suppressed reports but not maltreatment itself. Furthermore, services in CES seem to have been shifted toward the provision of emergency care with an apparent reduction in the intensity and duration of nonemergency services. The research design fails to measure the effects of this reemphasis on children who are in care or on those who have received less care. Yet if cost is a decisive criterion, then it is apparent that at least the Nashville taxpayer was better off with CES.

More important, demonstration effects may have accounted for much of the reported change. During such a short research period, the CES experiment may have taken advantage of unusual worker motivation and the ephemeral volition of local citizens. Workers may have been particularly attentive to project guidelines, discouraging unwanted reports or petitions. For example, the creation of "delinquency records" is notoriously reactive to program motivations.[2] Furthermore, during its short duration the project may have tapped into a limited local supply of emergency foster parents that may quickly become depleted, with unfortunate consequences for the number of very young children who need to be institutionalized. A demonstration needs to be measured after its novelty has worn off and its operation becomes routine for residents, workers, service recipients, and evaluators.

In the end, CES may have demonstrated little more than the possibility that motivated workers can follow instructions, whatever their consequences, in fulfilling mandated social goals. CES was designed to realize the community's imperative to reduce services and lower costs. Those goals were incarnated in the new CES system. CES workers were recruited and trained to fulfill those goals; their job performance was monitored; and, with predictable results, they produced effects that endorsed CES's stakes. Without directly measuring the outcomes of the children themselves, Burt

2. Lerman (1975) reanalyzed Palmer's claims that his project in the community care of delinquents reduced their criminality. Lerman argued that the apparent decline in Palmer's measure of delinquent behavior was probably the simple result of his staff's decision to sanction the adolescents with the same sort of restrictions as detention but refer to it as something else, thus avoiding the necessity of creating a "delinquency record" that would undermine the success of their project.

and Balyeat's "cost/benefit" evaluation lacks crucial evidence of the denominator. Nevertheless, the demonstration's success in reducing removal was warmly received by the permanency planning movement as early support for the plausibility of family preservation.

The political tendency to accept efficiency gains as proof of effectiveness is facilitated by faulty research. When two outcomes are equivalent, the less expensive is more desirable. Skepticism is smothered by evidence that the cheaper alternative actually appears to be more effective. In this way, compliant research like CES produces a melodrama of social experimentation that flatters the nation's decision to constrain its public commitments on grounds that no harm has been done and important social goals are achieved.

Similar to CES, a Second Chance for Families (SCF) (Jones 1985; Jones, Neuman, and Shyne 1976) focused on reducing the number of entries into the child welfare system, particularly long-term foster care. Rather than providing emergency care per se, beginning in 1974 SCF offered a range of "intensive" social services, notably counseling, for as long as one year. The increment for intensive care in the experimental group cost about two thousand dollars per child more than care for a child in the control group.

The experiment employed a randomized evaluative design to increase the credibility of its findings. However, the authors themselves point out that blinding was impossible and that the caseworkers were frequently aware of the status of their cases in the project: "There were occasional reports of workers, disappointed because a particular case was not selected for the intensive services, vowing to provide extraordinary service to a control case. . . . [W]ith the impossibility of concealing the identity of the control cases, they were subject to influence from many directions" (Jones, Neuman, and Shyne 1976:18).

The research relied on caseworkers and administrative data for information about family and child functioning. However, information was collected differently for experimental and for control cases. The authors conclude that

> the comparability of the data from the Outcome Schedules for experimental and control cases may well be questioned. It hardly needs to be said that the retrospective summary of service for the control group is likely to be a good deal less accurate than the compilation from the Monthly Service Schedules on experimental cases. (Jones, Neuman, and Shyne 1976:24)

Moreover, the two sets of caseworkers may well have had different motivations and attitudes toward the project. In the end, treatment integrity —

the methodological necessity for subjects to receive the care that was intended—cannot be assured. As a result, the project cannot certify that the experimental group received different services than the control group. This difference justified SCF's reason for being in the first place.

The project enrolled two types of cases that might benefit from services to either "prevent" or "rehabilitate." The preventive cases included children who "were awaiting placement away from home, were believed to be in imminent need of placement, or had already been placed on a temporary basis"; rehabilitative cases included "children already in long-term foster care or now home following long-term care and at risk of early reentry" (Jones, Neuman, and Shyne 1976:19).

Eligibility was restricted to children under fourteen years of age who had at least one parent at home and who could benefit from intensive service. This judgment of potential benefit was left up to the professional and implicit judgment of project staff, who were cognizant of the possibility that families might not receive more than six months of care. Nevertheless, the authors provide a sense that potential benefit was related to the severity of the families' presenting problems. That is, those families with fewer problems were apparently judged as more amenable to intensive services than those with many and severe problems. Put in terms of a Mad Hatter triage, those with apparently the least need received the most care.

The average length of service for both groups was about eight and one-half months,

> but those in the demonstration program received a great deal more service than those in the regular programs. The experimental cases received many more service contacts than the control cases; twice as many interviews were held with the mothers and four times as many contacts were made with collaterals . . . more types of service than the control cases, with the central service of casework counseling supplemented by a variety of practical services. (Jones, Neuman, and Shyne 1976:121)

A greater percentage of the experimental group than the control group appeared to receive services (e.g., counseling, financial assistance, medical care, help with housing, and family life education), and particularly in the case of counseling, the service was reportedly more intensive. However, the differences were modest, usually less than twenty percentage points, while 95 percent of the experimental group and 81 percent of the control group received counseling. Indeed, SCF was an experiment in counseling and referral more than in intensive social services. Yet the problem of treatment integrity is exacerbated by large majorities of both groups receiving the essential service and by the failure to accurately measure the receipt of subsequent services. Parenthetically, the caseworkers reported that counseling was the service that contributed most to progress; this is not surprising since caseworkers provided this service. The authors report this finding without any humor.

In the end, SCF endorsed the effectiveness of intensive services. In contrast with the control group, experimental group children spent twenty-four fewer days in foster care over the project year; fewer spent any time in foster care (52% vs. 60%); more who were at home initially were still at home (93% vs. 82%); more who were initially in foster care were returned home (47% vs. 38%); more had improved (62% vs. 52%). Six months after the project ended, the early success of the project had almost doubled, with 78 percent of the experimental group children compared with 60 percent of the control group children living at home.

However, after five years during which the experimental group had absorbed a median amount of nineteen months of services, the difference had narrowed to only 7 percent; 82 percent of the experimental group and 75 percent of the control were living with their parents, a relative, or could not be found in the files. Moreover, 66 percent of the experimental group children and 54 percent of the control group children had not utilized foster care during the five year follow-up (Jones 1985).[3]

It is notable that SCF achieved its largest gains in the softest areas of its judgments. The experimental group mothers improved more than control group mothers (59% vs. 36%). The emotional climate in the home favored the experimental group (62% vs. 36%). However, the putative improvements in maternal control and the home climate, often the process goals of counseling, apparently did not transfer to a similarly large success in reunification. Still, SCF boasted of an impressive financial success, projected lifetime savings of $1.8 million that would have been spent on foster care for experimental group children in the absence of the project.

Yet these are not impressive findings and the cost savings need to be evaluated against the actual condition of the children as well as the appearance of largely equivalent outcomes after five years. Rather than establishing the value of intensive services, small and transitory as it may be, SCF remains vulnerable to a variety of challenges to its study design. First, data were generated differently for the experimental and control groups, undermining treatment integrity and the reported differences between them. Indeed, at numerous points, caseworker bias in transmitting the aspirations of the demonstration seems manifest. Second, the control group appears to be more debilitated and therefore less amenable to reunification; "the mothers in the control cases had more functioning problems (5.5 vs. 4.9),

---

3. The five-year data are reported on approximately half the initial group, the New York City subsample.

and more of the children in the control group than in the experimental group were considered to be facing imminent placement (21% vs. 15%), rather than placement within 6 months (25% vs. 34%)" (Jones, Neuman, and Shyne 1976:120).

In addition, reunification may have resulted not from increased services and improved family functioning but from the decisions by caseworkers who were committed to the demonstration goals, particularly SCF's imperative to reunite families. The caseworkers may simply have taken greater risks with reunification among experimental children than control children, invoking the provision of relatively superficial services to justify their decisions. Without a hands-on, objective evaluation of the outcomes of the children there is little to contradict the cynical view that the project simply justified neglect on grounds that its interventions might provide somewhat better outcomes and save money. But these conclusions were not substantiated. Instead SCF relied on the uncorroborated evaluations of the workers themselves, a group that might well have perceived their own interests to lie along the line of the recorded success of the experimental children. Indeed, rather than the curative ability of experimental interventions, zealous workers in a crusade against objective accountability may have counterfeited the positive outcomes, however insubstantial, of the child welfare demonstrations.

Finally, the authors conclude from a separate regression analysis that the favorable outcomes of the SCF are more likely under specific conditions: (1) if the problems reside in the parents or the environment and not the child; (2) if the mother's attitude is positive toward the return of the child to the home; and (3) if her ability to care for her child is not severely disordered. This reduces to a pointless cliché that success is most likely when the problems are least severe. Yet the difficulties of the child welfare system emerge from the cases on the other end of the spectrum where families are severely disordered and when children have already been deeply harmed.

Why was the experiment allowed to proceed with such a large number of serious methodological problems? The threats to the internal validity of the research were apparent at the beginning of the demonstration. A good case should have been make for aborting the experiment before so many people were inconvenienced in the pursuit of illusory outcomes. Yet following a common pattern, this group of canny researchers opted to continue the demonstration without the ability to ensure the credibility of the research. The project itself emerges as an adventure in neglect, an experiment with truth that stoked enthusiasm for the Act of 1980 and its underlying professional dogmatism that cosmetic interventions are sufficient to achieve important social goals. A less committed summary of SCF suggests that even when labeled intensive, social services and casework counseling, in particular, make little difference in securing family reunification.

Also in pursuit of permanency, the Oregon Project (Emlen et al. 1978; Emlen et al. 1976; Lahti 1982; Pike 1976) offered services to reduce the number of children drifting in foster care by increasing the number of permanent exits, notably to adoption. The Oregon Project assumed that there were many children in foster care who would be adopted if specific barriers were overcome. "The project addressed the backlog of children whose status in foster care was indeterminate, drifting, and vague, focusing sharply on the goal of achieving an alternative to foster care that had greater prospects for permanence" (Emlen et al. 1977:1). In particular, the project sought to free children for adoption by terminating parental rights when there was little likelihood of reunification. However, in the course of reviewing cases, the prospect of reunification itself was reopened with the result of increasing the likelihood of reunification even when it was initially seen as implausible. "Some parents, when directed to appropriate resources, and supported and assisted by the caseworker, developed renewed motivation for parenting and were able to regain their children."

The three-year project screened twenty-three hundred foster children in Oregon to identify those most amenable to permanent placements. Five hundred and nine children were identified as both unlikely to be reunited with their parents and likely to be adopted. The project hired social workers and an attorney and drew on existing community agencies, particularly the Metropolitan Public Defender. They screened cases, developed permanency plans, and provided a range of social services to implement the permanency goals. In the cases judged appropriate for adoption, the termination of parental rights was aggressively sought through the courts.

Outcomes measured four years after the project began were quite impressive. Of the 509 children selected by the project, 52 percent were adopted and 27 percent were returned to their parents (Emlen et al. 1977:4). Moreover, these dispositions saved about four thousand months of foster care that would have cost over one million dollars during the course of the project and much more afterward.

The study did not incorporate a randomized control group. However, Lahti et al. (1978) later compared the placement dispositions of project children to two other groups: half of the children considered but not accepted into the project and a randomly selected group of children under twelve years of age who were in foster care in Oregon for at least one year.[4]

---

4. Somehow the average age of this sample whose upper limit was less than 12 was reported as over 11 years (137.385 months) (Lahti et al. 1978:appendix B2).

The group of considered children "had all the characteristics required for inclusion in the project but were excluded either because the action necessary for permanent placement was straightforward and did not require project intervention, or because the project caseload to which the child might be transferred was already filled" (3.1). Presumably this group would provide a near control for project children amenable for adoption while the group of foster children under twelve would provide a comparison for the remaining children who were difficult to adopt. Both of the comparison groups received customary state care.

Lahti and colleagues also made an unusually great effort to measure the quality of placements and outcomes through a series of detailed, structured questionnaires and interviews conducted by specially hired project staff. The data were taken from subsamples of adoptive parents, foster parents, and the children. Unfortunately, the information was gathered only once, at which time the respondents were asked to recall earlier conditions.

Lahti et al. (1978) reported less success for the project than Emlen et al. (1977): 66 percent vs. 79 percent in permanent placements. However, the experimental group and the two comparison groups were not at all equivalent, differing demographically and biographically; adjustments for age alone, since project children were considerably younger than those in the other groups, reduce the reported findings considerably, depriving the Oregon experiment of its theatrical importance.

The permanency placement rate of project children was 23 percent higher than the group of children considered but not selected and 20 percent higher than the group of children under twelve but in foster care for at least one year. About one-quarter of both project children and children under the age of twelve who had been in care at least one year were reunited with their families. The authors claim this is a remarkable success for the project since its caseload was drawn from those deemed unlikely to be reunited. However, placement misjudgments at this magnitude together with the age differentials among groups call attention to initial selection criteria. It is worth speculating that the criteria of adoptability—for example, younger children—were consistently favored and that the likelihood of return home, a subjective judgment to begin with, may have been consistently bent to favor positive project outcomes. As a result, it seems likely that many children may have been included in the project who would have been reunited in any case.

Lahti et al. further report that the project was approximately 10 percent more successful in achieving adoption than customary state services (received by the other two groups). But this is hardly remarkable considering the age differentials between the two groups and the project's screening criteria. More to the point, there was no statistically significant difference between adoption success among project children and considered children. This by itself severely restricts any claim to success.

It is startling, however, that age differences exceeded four years between project children and the sample of foster children under twelve and almost six years in comparison with the sample of considered but unselected children. The authors' own adjustments for age knocks out all subgroup differences: "The overall effect was that the project placed approximately the same number in permanent placements in this age group [the older children who were compared in this analysis] as customary casework activity." Still they defiantly maintain that "the project appears to have been more successful than regular [state] activity in placing younger children" (Emlen et al. 1977:4.2n). Moreover, the project was not able to ensure any greater stability in the placements themselves than any of the comparison groups. To the contrary, 20 percent of its reunifications failed whereas only 9 percent of reunifications failed among the group of children under twelve. These are not insubstantial recidivism rates, particularly considering that they accumulated within only eighteen months.

The quality of the outcomes is particularly important in this project since the authors acknowledge that when children were reunited with their parents a palpable risk was often taken.

> It was sometimes questionable whether the parents met standards for a minimum sufficient level of functioning as parents, but the children were returned anyway, because evidence was lacking to terminate their rights in court. Project staff found the decision to return children to marginally adequate parents less difficult, however, when the children had formed no strong ties to substitute parents during their years in foster care. The project operated under a heavy sense of responsibility to exhaust all reasonable opportunities to return a child to his biological parents. (Emlen et al. 1977:3)

Nevertheless, Lahti and colleagues (1978) are surprisingly reticent in providing quality scores of outcomes for the different comparison groups of children.[5] They do not report on the outcomes of project children who are returned home in comparison with any other group. It is remarkable, however, that when conflating the experience of all three groups, the children returned home were substantially less well off than children in foster care, again questioning the wisdom of the reunifications.

The authors do, however, go to great lengths in trying to explain the

---

5. Appendix table C.5 is one of the few presentations of the means of the interview and questionnaire items by group. It does not seem to contain any large or systematic differences among groups.

factors that contribute to better outcomes for the children without regard to the experience of the project children themselves. They reach a very flat finding that permanency predicts a large portion of the child's adjustment or, better said, that the reportedly permanent commitments of parents (usually adoptive parents in this study) to children predict better outcomes for the children. However, Lahti et al. come to the remarkable conclusion that the placement the child is in has little to do with the perception of permanency. This implies that the formal preferences of the permanency planning movement for adoption and reunification may not be valuable. It also recalls earlier criticism of disposition as an adequate measure of actual outcomes.

Still, the conditions that produce parental devotion may be more related to the children (perhaps youth together with physical and emotional health) than to the efforts of the Oregon Project. The authors fail to demonstrate that the Oregon Project created commitments to permanency at any greater rate than customary state services. In general, the literature has not demonstrated that these bonds with children can be husbanded in any fashion other than foraging for the society's extraordinarily limited supply of quality surrogate parents.

The Oregon Project, in spite of its self-regard, is hardly a success. It produced only a slightly better record of permanent placements than customary state care, an increase that does not seem to justify the risks it took in reuniting children with marginal parents. Moreover, almost all of its slight gains can be attributed to the age of the children, suggesting perhaps that the criteria for inclusion in the experiment had more to do with placement than the services it rendered. Its intense efforts to explain the quality of the outcomes did not endorse the project but simply reprised the unremarkable value of commitment between parents and children. Nevertheless, the Oregon Project put a political gloss on the reality of care by again underwriting the comforting fiction that trifling professional interventions can improve the welfare of children while also saving the public money.

The two-year Alameda experiment (Stein, Gambrill, and Wiltse 1978) tested the ability to achieve permanency through the provision of intensive services to birth parents. Four permanent outcomes were defined: reunification with parents, adoption, guardianship, and long-term foster care. The project's second goal was to evaluate the effectiveness of case management, the central service that it provided to parents. Case management employed "behavioral intervention methods . . . to resolve identified problems" (43). The study was trumpeted as a scientific breakthrough in the provision of "evidence about the outcomes of, and relative costs and benefits of, social service programs" (Gilbert and Specht 1978).

The study initially attempted an experimental design, although its departures from randomization in the end reduce the research to a quasi experiment. The authors were members of the social work faculty at the prestigious University of California, Berkeley. The experiment selected 428 children who conformed to four criteria: they were under sixteen years of age; at least one of their parents resided in the county; they were in family foster care; and no decision had been made about their future. The children were assigned within the Alameda County Social Service Department either to one of three experimental units or to the control unit. However, the assignment was not random. Rather, workers were "asked to volunteer cases from their active files" (Stein, Gambrill, and Wiltse 1978:44). Volunteered cases constituted 54 percent of the 227 members of the experimental group and fully 66 percent of the control group. It is also notable that 58 percent of the experimental group were six years or younger compared with only 31 percent of the control group. On the other side only 14 percent of the experimental group were over twelve compared with fully 22 percent of the control group. In the end, the experimental group contained newer and younger cases than the control group. Moreover, five of the experimental group caseworkers but none of the control group workers were employed through the project itself.

The outcomes of the study were again impressive. More of the experimental group children (56%) than control group children (34%) were reunified with their parents or adopted or in the process of reunification and adoption. A much greater percentage of the control group children (44%) than experimental group children (14%) were in long-term foster care. The authors attribute these large differences to the case management techniques, particularly the behavioral contracting methods, employed by the experimental group workers.

The largest threat to the credibility of the study's findings resulted from the authors' failure to justify the outcomes. They took no direct measure of the conditions of the children, electing to accept the dispositions as implicit evaluations of quality: restoration and adoption are good and better than long-term foster care, which is better than guardianship and drifting. Yet restoration to marginal families and troublesome adoptions are not favorable outcomes, especially if they are permanent; from the perspective of the child they may be far inferior to high-quality group foster care. Curiously, the one-year follow-up research, again simply a description of dispositions, was not reported differentially for control and experimental groups.

It is notable that the control group achieved a *higher* degree of permanency (reunifications, adoptions, *and* long-term foster care) than the experimental group. At the end of the intervention period, 30 percent of the experimental group cases and only 21 percent of control group cases were either closed in an unplanned manner or still open (i.e., no disposition decision had been made). Without truly comparable groups and detailed assessments of the conditions of the children, the meaning of the study's outcomes remain ambiguous and indeterminate. Yet it is quite possible that the control group outcomes eclipsed those of the experimental group.

Moreover, if the cases represented the underlying caseload or if the control services typified customary care, then far more control cases—perhaps more than half—should have still been open after one year of service. But the great number of permanency outcomes in the control group may suggest a placebo effect. That is, the control group workers may have thought or even tried to provide special care geared toward permanency. This seems a very likely consequence of collegial, quotidian discussions among the workers within the study agency that may have transmitted the project goals to control group workers while dispelling any mystique of case management. The differences in the types of permanent outcomes may have simply been the result of different needs within the experimental and control groups. Thus the similarity of outcomes may well undercut the claims of case management and behavioral methods. It is quite conceivable that the experiment's special training in behavioral methods had only fictive effects.

The findings become shakier on other grounds. Caseworkers volunteered their cases. In recognition of the five project workers in the three experimental units, the volunteered cases there probably differed from those volunteered by county workers to the control group. The large age differentials between the groups and the larger proportion of new cases in the experimental groups suggest that movement out of foster care may have been more easily accomplished for experimental group children. By itself the fact that many of them had just entered care predicts relatively quick placement.[6]

With this in mind, it is impossible to attribute the success of the experimental groups to the workers' techniques and not to the conditions and characteristics of the children. Furthermore, the reunifications may have emerged simply as a result of the workers' decisions (and the propensity for risk-taking that the project may have engendered) and not as a result of having achieved any higher level of functioning among parents. Similarly, without comparable groups, the greater proportion of hours that experimental workers spent with parents in contrast with the control workers (who spent the largest proportion of their hours on foster placements)

6. As noted in the previous chapter, many children utilize the child welfare system for a very short time. It is suggestive that for all the measures the authors take in comparing experimental and control groups, they fail to compare them by the length of time the children had previously spent in care.

may be a tribute to the different possibilities of the children themselves. Furthermore, a demonstration effect, produced by project workers who are highly motivated to produce the goals of the project during a relatively short period of intense scrutiny, may account for the outcomes. These results could probably not be achieved over the long haul of routine agency operation nor might they be replicated by agencies that do not act in the melodrama of social experimentation.

Finally, it is not clear to what extent the Alameda project cases were representative of cases in the County, California, or the nation. The selection criteria of the project suggest that its results may in the end pertain only to the very small percentage of foster children for whom reunification and adoption are both possible and desirable.

This is incomplete, poorly conducted, and in the end factitious research. The Alameda project created a faddish enthusiasm for behavioral contracting and case management that has captured social policy and social work for the past twenty years. The child welfare system might have avoided these false convictions by simply insisting that case workers reunite more children with their parents. However, with such frank instructions, the culture and its program managers would not be able to mask America's indifference as rational, scientific social policy. Notwithstanding Fein and Maluccio's (1984) bland observation that the foster care system might not be so bad for its charges, there appears to be little concern with the children themselves. If indeed Fein and Maluccio are correct (and they are probably not), then the limited harmfulness of foster care is more a tribute to the indestructibility of youth than testimony to the mercy, grace, and generosity of America.

In spite of their flawed methods and frequently contradictory findings, four of five notable experiments—CES, SCF, Oregon, and Alameda but not the much ignored Sherman et al.—marched brazenly under banners of social progress and scientific advance to endorse the provisions of the Act of 1980. However, a prudent skepticism should have denied them any standing before policy. A public made credulous by its desire for less collective responsibility accepted the research in order to reconcile its low-tax ambitions with its sense of duty. The 1970s might yet emerge as the golden age of social service research—a time when the helping professions created the principal myths of a pernicious liberalism.

After the Act of 1980: Experimental Support
for Child Welfare Interventions

Although the amount of drift was exaggerated by the early research, the major program demonstrations that boosted the feasibility of the Act of

1980 suggested that a variety of interventions could greatly reduce child welfare caseloads. As a consequence, the Act of 1980 was specifically legislated to reduce the number of children drifting in foster care by encouraging permanent placements and by mounting a preventive strategy through family preservation. Family preservation services were given a separate boost in the Family Preservation and Family Support Services Act of 1994.

The Act of 1980 provided for services to reunify children in long-term care with their families, to increase adoptions, and to prevent placement before children became long-term dependents of public care. Family reunification and family preservation services along with more explicitly psychotherapeutic child welfare services reflect the basic, socially efficient tenets of liberalism and its reliance on the social sciences for intervention truths. These programs, at the center of contemporary social work, are also uniformly superficial in spite of their authors' claims—the essential "intensive" service is supervision of care and of the families by professional caseworkers. They cost perhaps a few thousand dollars per family; provide care over relatively short periods of time; and ignore both theoretically and practically the underlying social conditions that give rise to the need for child welfare placements.

Not only do the social problems associated with child welfare placements seem impervious to superficial program interventions, but the social sciences have routinely failed to identify the causal relations among the conditions that produce social problems. The experience with family reunification, family preservation, and a number of other program initiatives encouraged by the Act of 1980—notably treatment foster care and foster parent training—underpin this grim assessment of programmatic liberalism's ineffectiveness and underscore its ideological role in justifying social neglect.

Family Reunification

Family reunification encompasses the specific programmatic initiatives as well as the conditions of foster care that have been encouraged by the Act of 1980 to restore children with their parents. They include mandated case reviews, efforts to improve the ability of parents to care for their children, and interventions to improve the ability of children to remain with their parents.

> Reunification programs focus on the provision of services that both promote the full reentry of children to their homes and, if full reentry is not appropriate, a level of family contact that maintains a child's bond to and involvement with her/his family. It may take time to accomplish reunification and therefore services that create mechanisms for children to

94 Experiments with Truth

make frequent home visits are an integral part of the reunification process. (Fraser et al. 1996:338)

At least on the surface, that is, judged by dispositions, the Act of 1980 does appear to have increased the rates of family reunification. In 1982 about 39 percent of children had permanency planning goals of reunification; in 1989 the comparable figure was about 60 percent. However, again, these figures are misleading by themselves, failing to adjust for disruptions and failing to report the actual percentage that were reunified. Still, permanency planning does not seem to have been achieved for an enormous number of children unless one accepts the questionable and professionally convenient irony that the great increase in foster care itself somehow realizes the expectations for permanency. Yet both foster care and kinship care are frequently failures measured against any reasonable standard of modern decency.

Apart from these simple conclusions, the conditions and dynamics of the child welfare system have not been well described by the research. There is still no credible or complete national data reporting system in place; moreover, the literature offers only snapshots of care taken at widely spaced times and in just a few locations. Indeed, there is no evidence to dispel the suspicion that for the majority of children, lengths of stay in foster care as well as the numbers of reunifications may have changed little since Maas and Engler (1959) declared a crisis of children lost in care. Yet the enormous increase in foster care since the late 1980s together with the declining proportion of exits suggest that successful family reunification may actually be decreasing.

The examination of the "intensive" programs that were designed to reunify families hints at the gravity of problems besetting the public child welfare system. These programs mark a level of restricted service that routinely fails to reunify families even while their cost represents an investment in care above the funding tolerances of the public for child welfare generally.

The Casey Family Services (CFS) program (Fein and Staff 1991, 1993) was instituted as a three-year demonstration program beginning during 1989 in Maine, Vermont, and Connecticut. CFS offered intensive "family-oriented, home-based, clinical case management" to children in foster care who were judged capable of being restored to their families if intensive services were provided. These families were ambivalent about the return of their children yet they were not actively abusive. "In many cases" the referring state had made the determination that its customary services were not adequate to reunify the family. However, "to be accepted into the . . . program, the biological family must be willing to work with the reunification team in formulating a service agreement that incorporated goals and plans for reunification" (Fein and Staff 1993:34).

The services were provided by a two-person team—a social worker and a family support worker—who carried fewer than five cases and met with each recipient family three or four times per week in their homes. The goal of CFS was to restore the children to their families within six months, although services could continue for up to two years after reunification (Fein and Staff 1991). The emphasis of the service was on

> "parenting the parents" to help them in turn to nurture their children. Workers provide training in parental skills, mental health counseling, respite care, coaching in homemaking, budgeting assistance, help with job training and apartment-hunting, transportation, and support for substance abuse treatment. The work is focused on client strengths that can be mobilized to pursue the goals and plans that are the basis of the service provision. (Fein and Staff 1993:27)

CFS brings friendly visiting down from the attic but unfortunately fails to improve its efficacy. After two years of operation, CFS had been able to reunify only 38 percent of its highly screened cases and seven of these were returned to foster care, producing an even lower success rate of 28 percent. Indeed, the three states had referred only 117 children to CFS and CFS accepted but 80 of them. The selected children were young, 78 percent under five years of age.

Fein and Staff (1993) report that successful reunification was frequently associated with the parent's motivation. This thunderously unremarkable conclusion, however, is the product of a research design incapable of testing the authors' hope that the intensive clinical casework improved the motivation of parents. The program failed to employ any comparison group, let alone the randomized controls that are required to prove causation, thus impeding an assessment of the number of similar children who would have been reunified in the absence of intensive services. Rather than attesting to the therapeutic powers of clinical casework, CFS's modicum of success might have been due simply to the surveillance that the home visits provided over the behavior of lackluster parents. The more important test of permanence takes place after the outsiders—the social workers—are withdrawn from the reunified homes.

Still, the authors attempt to weight their findings with the observation that the "typical parent the program worked with was a single mother of several children, who was unemployed or underemployed, without financial resources, often homeless or living in a temporary shelter, a substance abuser, and a victim of abuse either currently, as a child, or both" (Fein and Staff 1993:34). However, the program did not typically succeed with the typical parent. To the contrary, its low success rate of 28 percent raises the suspicion that the demonstration contained a small number of prime candidates for reunification who may not have needed CFS. The researchers never address this obvious possibility in any of their analyses.

In the end, then, a creamed study population decidedly unrepresentative of the caseloads in three states received intensive clinical casework of unproven value and with unknown effects. The researchers failed either to establish a baseline of comparison or to justify the importance of their demonstration. More important they failed either to dispel the naive suspicion that the services were unneeded in the first place or to measure the actual quality of the children's experience in the reunified families.

Nevertheless, Fein and Staff (1993) insist upon their success: "The experience of the Casey Family Services Reunification program demonstrates that families with multiple and serious problems can be reunified if a program has the resources to offer intensive services" (34). This is the sort of conclusion that inspires dreams of professionalism in clinical social work, but it does not provide a justification for care at even the weak levels advocated by contemporary structuralists (e.g., Pelton and Lindsey). To the contrary, it undercuts even the parsimony of current, inadequate levels of care.

The Utah experiment, Family Reunification Services (FRS), spent even less money than CFS on reunification services while apparently achieving a greater success (Fraser et al. 1996).[7] The pool of foster children in four districts in Utah were screened to select those who could safely return home if services were provided. A randomly selected group of these cases was then randomly assigned either to an experimental group that received FRS for ninety days or to a nontreatment control group that provided only customary state care. FRS included counseling and drug treatment, family skills training, concrete services (e.g., food, housing, employment, health and mental health care), and income support. The FRS strategy included a substantial range of concrete services along with clinical counseling. Cases were followed for one year after the completion of the services.

Fifty-five of fifty-seven children in the FRS group (96.5%) compared with only twenty-eight of fifty-three children in the control (52.9%) were reunited with their families. However, during the one-year follow up, 72.7 percent of the experimental reunifications succeeded as compared with 89.3 percent of the control reunifications. Therefore, by the end of the re-

---

7. The tendency to produce more with less recalls the facility with which psychotherapy has concocted evidence that treatment has become more effective as interventions have become shorter. Logically, then, the most effective treatment is the shortest with a true panacea delivered in no time at all. Fortunately for psychotherapy, it is saved from extinction by the inadequacy of its own research.

search, FRS achieved reunification for 70.2 percent of its cases compared with 47.2 percent who received only customary state care.

Fraser et al. (1996) conclude that "relatively brief and intensive family-centered services can significantly affect reunification rates" (355). However, they ignore simple administrative fiat as an alternative explanation. It is obvious that the FRS workers took greater risks than control workers and the price for their success was paid in part by the children whose reunifications failed. Penalties for administrative enthusiasms that are paid by children are not lightly dismissed or easily discounted against the authors' boast to have saved sixty dollars for each day of reduced foster care. Furthermore, the success of FRS is difficult to attribute to any specific strategy since its intervention package included clinical as well as concrete services. Indeed, the small true differences between the experimental and control groups might well hint at the limitations of income and housing supports to achieve reunification. Furthermore, as the authors acknowledge, Utah may not be typical of the nation: it may have contained only "a residual group of cases which required little more than emphasizing reunification—rather than long term out-of-home care" (356). These residual cases might well not exist after the program was in operation for more than a few months, with the result of further depressing potential differences between recipients of FRS services and recipients of customary state care.

Finally, in spite of random assignment, the experimental and control groups differed consistently along important criteria. The control group seemed to contain more debilitated children with a variety of characteristics that would make them harder to place. Compared with FRS children, control group children were more frequently male, minority, older, expelled from school, drawn from residential placements, less educated, and exhibiting behavioral disorders. It is also suggestive in Mormon Utah that 67.7 percent of the experimental group's caretakers but only 55.2 percent of the control group's caretakers professed regular participation in the Mormon church. While few of these differences were statistically significant by themselves, taken together they might well begin to explain the reported outcomes (Walton 1991).

The Illinois Family Reunification Program (FRP) also provided both concrete and counseling services to families who were judged by protective service investigators or caseworkers as likely candidates for reunification (Rzepnicki, Schuerman, and Johnson 1997:231). FRP services included cash assistance, "provision of food, furniture, or household goods, utility benefits, day care, homemakers, and baby sitters," as well as a variety of counseling services and case management. The services were designed to be limited to six months and intensive, requiring "frequent in-person contact with families and at least weekly visitation between parents and their children." Still, almost half of FRP cases were receiving care for longer than six months. Families averaged more than two hours per week of casework in addition to other services. Furthermore,

> Caseworkers have small caseloads, usually between four and eight cases, which permits them to meet frequently with families and to be available at all times. They often work in teams with homemakers or case aides. Initial plans called for specially recruited foster parents who would be active members of the treatment team. (Rzepnicki, Schuerman, and Johnson 1997:232)

In addition to the judgment of workers, families that were accepted into the FRP program met objective criteria designed to screen for those who were most amenable to reunification. FRP families needed to "be relatively new to the child welfare system," with fewer than four reports for maltreatment. Moreover, under the assumption that reunification is easier with both younger children and those in care for a short time, selected families had at least one child under age thirteen in placement for six months or less.

The project did not employ a random control, although it did construct a matched comparison group from the administrative records of foster children during a comparable period of time. However, as the authors note, the two groups may well have been quite different. Indeed, the fact that FRP had "difficulties in keeping program slots full" and therefore could not construct a control from "overflow" cases suggests that the treatment group may have exhausted the easy possibilities for reunification. Thus the results in Illinois as in Utah may well inflate estimates of the proportion of the foster care caseload for whom reunification is a likely outcome.

In the end, FRP reported outcomes that seemed to disappoint state officials: 45 percent of its children were returned home within six months of referral, 48 percent within nine months, and 53 percent within one year. Rates were lower in Chicago than downstate Illinois. FRP reunification rates eventually exceeded control rates by only 20 percent. Moreover, FRP recidivism, recalling the FRS experience, reached 28 percent after twenty-four months. Considering the likelihood that the control group contained a much more difficult caseload, the FRP results hardly paint a rosy prospect for reunification. And again, the research took no independent measures of the reunified situations of the children, which is particularly worrisome in light of its high recidivism rates.

The authors, who are attached to the prestigious social work program at the University of Chicago and to Chapin Hall, a renowned child welfare research center, state that concrete services were highly related to reunification.[8] However, since reunification was not a uniform outcome even within this highly screened group, it is questionable that the temporary provision of concrete services will have an extensive or consistent impact on reunification. The authors seem content with their results, refusing to commend either the permanent provision of truly intensive services in support of families or a far more extensive provision of very expensive long-term foster care in congregate settings as a permanent alternative to failed families. Rather than pointing to the failure of their minimal intervention, they choose to clutch to their organizational bosoms the redeeming belief that FRP recipient families "benefitted in ways not measured" even though reunification was not achieved.

Yet a less congratulatory conclusion seems more consistent with their data: FRP failed to identify the mix of services needed to restore families. The threshold of care required to reunify families may involve either a greater number and intensity of services than FRP provided or, alternatively, recognition of the difficulty of repairing dysfunctional families. This conclusion, however, would invite conflict with the State of Illinois, which funded the research. Professional prudence and other careerist motives camouflaged by the high-minded grandeur of social policy research tracks to self-serving conclusions that cushion the failures of contributing public agencies to fulfill their obligations.

HomeRebuilders in New York City capitated care in the fashion of health maintenance organizations (Wulczyn and Zeidman 1997). On the assumption that foster care agencies produce disposition outcomes as a result of their own corporate incentives, HomeRebuilders created a schedule of payments for agencies that achieved relatively permanent placements for their caseloads through reunification or adoption. Under the capitation plan, agencies would save money if they diverted relatively expensive foster care maintenance payments to services that reduced reentries to foster care. If successful, HomeRebuilders would realize the widely shared goal of delivering services to families in order to prevent future placements. In contrast, Wulczyn and Zeidman believed that the customary per diem method of reimbursing agencies created a counterproductive fiscal incentive for the foster care agency "to achieve a stable base of care days to support the established costs of operation, or to increase the base of care days to support the costs of an expanding operation" (263).

However, as with capitated health maintenance organizations, the danger always exists that effectiveness and quality of services will be relinquished for organizational profit. This is even more of a danger with foster children, since they are not free consumers who can shop around for

8. Yet they do not provide the measures of this relationship.

the best package of benefits. The exchange of foster children's interests for organizational interests would be indicated by injudicious reunifications with their parents, by inappropriate adoptions, or by deferring necessary returns to care after placement.

The evaluation of the project employed a randomized control drawn from each of the six private, participating agencies. The preliminary one-year findings of the demonstration are both incomplete and perhaps premature, but they are still troubling.[9] "Seventy-nine percent of the Home-Rebuilders children remained in care at the end of the first year compared with 85% of the children in the comparison group." The authors applaud themselves for this difference of only 6 percent: "Thus . . . the Home-Rebuilders programs successfully accelerated the discharge of children from foster care" (Wulczyn and Zeidman 1997:268).

Later reports will apparently rely on interviews with parents and the judgments of the project's caseworkers—hardly a basis for "objective indices"—to evaluate the conditions of the families and their children. Yet the very small gain of the HomeRebuilders groups can simply be attributed to the ephemeral enthusiasm of the demonstration staff and, more challenging to Wulczyn and Zeidman's claims, to the administrative emphasis placed on reunification. There is no evidence that capitation played a role, thus smothering any fire for simplistic organizational incentives as remedies for complex social problems.

Intensive services, such as they are, designed to achieve family reunification are much ado about nothing. Far from suggesting a promising solution for the problems of child welfare, the most credible evaluations of family reunification programs hint at only limited possibilities to enhance reunification through short-term and relatively superficial supportive services. A few hours of counseling, short-lived relief from the strains of poverty, and a bit better housing may be intensive compared with the vagaries of customary state services. However, these services are grossly inadequate to alleviate problematic situations or to change the dysfunctional behaviors of inadequate parents.

Yet the report of apparent success in experiments with intensive family reunification may have a perverse long-term political effect. The findings inappropriately discredit the current provision of care by suggesting that greater programmatic success at lower costs is possible through greater professional supervision, the essential component of each of the intensive packages of services. However, these inaccurate evaluations will also tend

---

9. The one-year report did not include descriptions of the experimental and control groups or procedures for obtaining "objective indices" of family functioning, which presumably would describe the actual situations and risks faced by the children.

to discourage any interest in providing adequate services when the impotence of current programmatic arrangements become obvious in spite of the literature. Because more services at least at the levels funded by legislation do not appear to produce better outcomes, the broader service component of child welfare may simply be seen as unnecessary, abetting American society's growing indifference to deprivation and inequality. The bogus claims of social service researchers neither soften the severity of public child welfare nor forestall the implacable public demands for lower taxes, less welfare, and a smaller public role.

The very goal of reunification is often questionable and twenty-five years of federal legislation may be misguided. The outcomes for children who are reunified with their parents may be worse than for children in long-term foster placements. Reunified children seem to have lower IQ scores (Fanshel and Shinn 1978), poorer social adjustment (Lahti et al. 1978), more haphazard school attendance (Leitenberg et al. 1981), more contact with the criminal justice system and greater emotional problems (Kinard 1982), and worse physical care and lower school achievement (Wald, Carlsmith, and Leiderman 1988). Indeed, enthusiasm for reunification may have a greater symbolic value in support of a chauvinistic notion of the American family than it does for the children themselves. Ironically, the reunified family is one of the few standards against which foster care compares favorably even while it provides an indictment of American compassion.

The reunification experiments also fail to address a compelling point of skepticism that administrative fiat—a mindless organizational imperative to reunify families—accounts for their outcomes. This alternative to intensive services as an explanation for increased reunification may supply a parsimonious public with an austere remedy for high caseloads in foster care: require greater reunifications. Particularly in the Utah situation, but also as a demonstration effect in all the other programs, bureaucratic imperatives may have been applied with a cruel and mindless disregard for the welfare of the children themselves; FRS may have achieved its unprecedented level of reunification by simply converting parental maltreatment into organizational malice, putting the child at risk while apparently reducing pressure on the taxpayer.

However, the researchers in Utah as elsewhere fail to protect themselves from this interpretation by taking steps to credibly measure the actual situations of placed children. Instead, the literature typically relies on interviews with parents and caseworkers—notoriously unreliable sources—for outcome assessments. Taken together, the compromises of the researchers and the many pitfalls of their research constitute professional decadence: in the hope of political favor, the self-interests of social service researchers overwhelm an obligation for credible research. The opera buffa of family reunification becomes tragedy in the more extensive efforts to preserve families.[10]

Family Preservation

In 1994 federal legislation gave family preservation programs a boost, authorizing $240 million by 1998 for the states to spend on these programs. But even before this legislation, states had been experimenting with service programs designed to prevent the dissolution of high-risk families and the subsequent out-of-home placement of their children. Homebuilders is one of the earliest and most popular family preservation programs but the literature also contains a substantial range of similar programs.

Commonly referred to as intensive family preservation services (IFPS), these programs share a number of characteristics: they are home-based; they provide various counseling and concrete services that the field at least considers to be intensive; and they are provided for relatively short periods of time, usually less than one year. Families *at imminent risk* of dissolution are referred for family preservation services, frequently during a crisis, the theory of the services being that early and intensive intervention will lower the need for protective and foster care services. In one description of Homebuilders,

> Therapists are on call twenty-four hours a day, seven days a week for a one-month period to help defuse the precipitating crisis and, further, to teach families new skills that will help to prevent the crisis from recurring. Almost all of the work we do with families takes place in the homes, neighborhoods and schools of our clients. We may work with a mother at home on housecleaning, see the teenage son at the local McDonald's and go with him to school to help assess what is making it so punishing for him and how the setting could be made more rewarding.
>
> Workers serve only two families at a time. They provide these families, as needed, with a wide range of services, including helping with basic needs such as food, shelter and clothing, and counseling regarding emotions and relationships. (Kinney et al. 1988:37)
>
> We think it's best for most families to learn to handle their own problems rather than continually relying on the state to rescue them when things get rough. Family preservation services reinforce tenacity, hard work, commitment and duty; they discourage avoidance, dependence, and hopelessness. (39)

10. Adoption is a limited but consistent option for public child welfare. Yet it does not seem to be capable of greatly reducing the number of children in care while disruption rates are considerable and probably undercounted. See Barth (1992) and Barth and Berry (1994).

After thirteen years of experience, the only group we are reluctant to
serve are parents who are so addicted to hard drugs that their entire lives
are focused on obtaining them and in surviving in very dangerous drug
cultures. (39)

Indeed, the revivalist intensity of practitioner belief in family preservation combines the idealized virtues of the family and civic responsibility,
psychic healing, the fashionable strengths perspective (a rage in social work
that competes with Norman Vincent Peale's inspirational hype), and the
mysticism of a social oneness. Bloom (1992) would probably define family
preservation as a variety of American religion with roots in both theology
and social experience. Few families are beyond help (salvation); "clients are
our colleagues" (populist humility); "it is our job to instill hope" (American optimism); "people are doing the best they can do" (the remission of
guilt), and so forth (Kinney et al. 1988:40–44).

Some of the evaluations of family preservation programs have been
sophisticated, incorporating large samples, randomized controls, and extensive data collection over relatively long follow-up periods. However,
many of the evaluations lack any controls and employ questionable measures of success.

The problem of targeting family preservation services has bedeviled all
evaluations. Indeed, high reported success rates in many projects—Homebuilders, for example, reported that 97 percent of its cases avoided placement three months after termination of services and 88 percent avoided
placement at one-year follow-up (Kinney et al. 1988:37)—could be attributed to provision of services to families whose children are not really at imminent risk of placement, that is, the families would not break up without
family preservation services. Because of the problem of targeting, a randomized nontreatment control or at least a randomized standard treatment
control is a crucial requirement of any evaluation design. For the same reason, evaluation methodologies are also obliged to prove that selected families are at imminent risk of dissolution or, in the absence of proving imminent risk, at least to carefully describe the conditions of serviced families.

When Homebuilders, among others, finesses the targeting problem by
subtly claiming that it is impossible to predict who will benefit from IFPS,
it is also undermining the initial justification for care (Kinney et al. 1988).
If family preservation proponents are to justify programs in terms of child
welfare placements, then family preservation programs must be proven to
prevent placement by maintaining families. Furthermore, if IFPS is to be
implemented as a humane alternative to placement and not simply a less

expensive form of care, then evaluations must also prove that children are not worse off by being maintained in their families.

The notion of IFPS is politically attractive. Rossi notes:

> Family preservation has features that attract supporters from a wide variety of backgrounds and interests. Fiscal conservatives are attracted by its claim to lower the costs of dealing with child abuse and neglect. Social conservatives like the idea of preserving families and strengthening family ties. Social workers like the promise it holds for lowered case loads and greater opportunities to provide services. Those who are opposed to the growth of state bureaucracies like the idea of contracting out social work services. It is not easy to be opposed to family preservation: If it works as advertised, it is clearly a fix that will do much to ameliorate one of our more troubling social problems. (Rossi 1994:462)

But are IFPS effective? Probably not. While a substantial amount of the research testifies to success, the studies are grievously flawed as credible evaluations. Moreover, a few studies, and customarily the better conducted ones, have found that IFPS is ineffective. Unfortunately, these studies are also methodologically flawed even while one of them, the evaluation of IFPS in Illinois, is among the most sophisticated experiments ever conducted of personal social services, comparing favorably with the best of the social experiments of the past thirty years.

The IFPS in Utah and Washington were both expressions of Homebuilders focused on preventing out-of-home placements among families at risk of imminent dissolution. As reported in *Families in Crisis,* these two programs were extensively evaluated by program advocates (Fraser, Pecora, and Haapala 1991). The research incorporated an overflow comparison group in Utah, but not a truly randomized control; the Washington experiment was uncontrolled with only before and after comparisons. Imminent risk of placement was assumed to exist when the referring agency reported plans to place a child within one week if IFPS were not provided. Eligibility for services was also dependent on reasonable assurances of safety for the child and the compliance of at least one parent in attending initial service interviews.

The authors report great success. At the end of services, and, more important, one year after intake, children in only 30 percent of the experimental families were placed (i.e., 70% of the families were preserved). In comparison with the Utah experimental group during the follow-up period, a greater proportion of children in the Utah overflow group were placed (85% vs. 41%) and their placements occurred in more restrictive settings. On the basis of information provided by parents and caseworkers it appears that IFPS improved the functioning of participants. "When the change scores of the other measures were examined . . . it was clear that participation . . . was highly correlated with improvements in the behavior of the children, the parenting repertoire of parents, and conditions in the home" (Fraser, Pecora, and Haapala 1991:148).

The change in behavior is all the more remarkable in light of the amount of service the participants actually received. In Washington, cases were closed after an average of thirty days during which participants received an average of only thirty-six hours of direct contact with workers. In Utah, the average case was closed after sixty-three days and thirty-nine hours of direct contact. The authors report an immense range of services and service tasks. However, the actual amount of care received by target families does not seem to sum up to a very intensive experience in spite of the authors' assertions. Indeed, if the findings are credible, they would mark an immense effect for relatively superficial care.

The authors take heart from their findings to endorse the expansion of IFPS. They even point to the outcomes in Washington State to suggest that IFPS can be targeted on the highest risk children. "Children of color targeted for placement in Washington State had a significantly higher chance of remaining at home during and after Homebuilders treatment than their white, non-Hispanic counterparts" (Fraser, Pecora, and Haapala 1991:302). Specific support for this finding comes from a weak multivariate analysis of "ethnic minority children"[11] who had a "significantly lower risk (−54.5%) of service failure when compared to white, non-Hispanic children" (217). Yet the largest portion of the Washington experiment's children of color (only 18% of the sample) was presumably Asian but not Filipino and not black or Hispanic. This select subgroup of Asian children may be unusual and perhaps much less needy than the largest portion of America's people of color, African Americans and Hispanics. Paradoxically, the authors also report the contradictory finding that "when the 12-month, child-based, follow-up data for Washington were analyzed, the placement rate for children of color was 22.7% versus 31.7 for white, non-Hispanic children. The difference, however, was not significant" (188).

The apparent success of the experiment needs to be discredited by its extensive and debilitating methodological problems, problems that the authors clearly perceive. The authors point to the absence of true randomized controls, limitations of their comparison group design, reactivity of measures, recall problems, limited measures of outcomes, and others.[12] In spite

11. Who are apparently not equivalent to "children of color."

12. These authors, while enthusiasts for intensive family preservation, are also very sophisticated methodologists and therefore they seem to knowingly overstate the meaning of their findings. Their other works are models of thoughtful consideration of the problems of

of their disclaimers to definitive research, throughout *Families in Crisis* as well as in some of their other publications (e.g., Pecora, Fraser, and Haapala 1992; Pecora et al. 1995; Pecora, Whittaker, and Maluccio 1992), the authors treat the findings as credible testimony that IFPS programs do in fact prevent out-of-home placements and certainly improve family functioning.

Nonetheless, the Utah and Washington experiences are very shaky support for the effectiveness of Homebuilders. To begin with, it is not at all clear that the families in Utah and notably Washington were either representative of families that have children placed or were truly at imminent risk of dissolution. Mean education attainment for the total sample was over twelve years; only 36 percent of the sampled families had single caretakers; 63 percent derived the major source of family income from jobs; the median family income was more than $10,000 (the poverty line for a family of four in 1989 was $12,674) while almost one-quarter of the sample had incomes over $20,000 per year. Only 30 percent of the sample relied on AFDC. Almost 45 percent of the sample appear to own their own homes.

Imminent risk was not assessed objectively. The referring agency's declaration that it intended to place the child within one week unless IFPS were provided may have been a device to secure services for favored clients. This may have led to a "net-widening" problem in targeting services (as discussed in the Illinois experiment below). Moreover, the authors acknowledge that "a number of control or comparison group studies (ours included) have found that not all children designated 'at risk of placement' are actually placed in the absence of intensive family preservation services" (Fraser, Pecora, and Haapala 1991:159–60). Fifteen percent of the overflow sample that could be traced were not placed. However, the overflow sample traced only two-thirds of its members and the suspicion is live that these were the least disabled. As a consequence, many more than 15 percent of the samples may not have been at risk of imminent placement, whereas placement prevention rates in the untreated Utah comparison group may have been much higher.

The overflow group may not have been constructed randomly. Fraser, Pecora, and Haapala report that it was to be composed of referrals that "met the criteria for acceptance but could not be served due to full therapist caseloads" (1991:65). However, the children in the overflow group appear to be very troubled, raising the possibility that therapists exercised

---

child welfare research. The ambiguity and distortions of research beg for political interpretations, particularly in situations such as these in which the researchers are aware of methodological limitations but still appear to manipulate professionally expedient findings.

some greater discretion in assigning cases to the overflow group than the research reports. The authors' attempt to adjust for the children's disabilities by comparing the overflow group with a matched subgroup of experimental children fails to adjust for other family characteristics such as the compliance of parents. It is notable that the matching procedures broke down on at least two important variables, family size and family structure. In any event, and not least because of an attrition of almost one-third, the overflow control does not constitute a convincing comparison.

The measures of improvement were collected from interviews with parents and caseworkers. As Rossi comments drily, "no social work program can be judged adequately by asking practitioners how well they are doing" (1991:465). In the same way, people who have been receiving services, and frequently without any requirement to pay for them, are not adequate judges of their workers or the effects of the services. Gratitude and perhaps a sense of obligation to report progress may well compromise their accuracy. Patient self-evaluations are problematic, notably in psychotherapeutic and counseling settings, since they may be influenced more by the conditions of treatment, for example, the warmth of the workers, than by consideration of verifiable behavioral change. Indeed, even the authors acknowledge the likelihood that their measures were reactive to the research situation, distorting reports of family relations. Accurate measurement of the outcome situations is particularly necessary in studies such as this one that assert on a priori grounds that maintenance of the family is preferable to placement. Furthermore, as in many other studies, the seemingly high rates of placement prevention may not have been due to services but rather to the project's ability to stiffen administrative reluctance to place children from the experimental IFPS groups.

In the end, it is not clear that Homebuilders succeeded in holding together families at risk of imminent dissolution or that this was a desirable outcome for the children. Moreover, the assessments of improved family functioning are highly suspect. The findings, such as they are, may also not be readily applicable to the troubled families that typically fall into the public child welfare system. Yet the study remains prominent—for its thoroughness and efforts although not its methodological rigor—among the group of investigations attesting to the effectiveness of IFPS (Halper and Jones 1981; Jones 1985; Lyle and Nelson 1983 as reported in Schuerman, Rzepnicki, and Littell 1994; Szykula and Fleischman 1985; Wood, Barton, and Schroeder 1988).

In contrast, the evaluation of IFPS in Illinois, Putting Families First (PFF), while methodologically stronger than the Utah and Washington experiment, reported far less favorable outcomes. PFF is probably the best of the small number of randomized controlled evaluations of IFPS and tends to corroborate their findings (Feldman 1990; McDonald and Associates 1990; Meezan and McCroskey 1996; Willems and DeRubeis 1981).

Meezan and McCroskey also report a tentative but still provocative finding from a stepwise logistic regression analysis that hints at the possibility of differential administrative controls over the children in experimental IFPS groups in comparison with controls: "placement decisions may be made differently for families receiving home-based services than for those receiving traditional child protective services" (1996:22). Oddly, their experimental group reported modest improvements in family functioning only after services had been terminated.

Putting Families First, the evaluative enterprise and not the auspices of the services themselves, set out to test whether family preservation services in Illinois produced better outcomes than the customary services provided through the Illinois Department of Child and Family Services (DCFS).[13] In pursuit of a scientifically credible study, PFF incorporated a classical, prospective experimental design: large samples, random selection and random assignment, multiple sites, multiple measures, follow-up, neutral measurement, and so forth. Service recipients and applicants were randomized either to the experimental condition in which family preservation services were provided or to the DCFS control at a variety of different sites throughout Illinois.

PFF's family preservation services were similar to many other family preservation programs. They were targeted on families at imminent risk of placement. PFF's experimental families received a median of 108 days of service, considerably more than the 90 days that were originally planned. "There is substantial evidence that the Family First program provided both a wider range and far more intensive service [to experimentals] than cases in the regular service group" (Schuerman, Rzepnicki, and Littell 1994:109). Workers reported that the average experimental recipient received 3.8 concrete services and 3.2 counseling services while controls received only 0.8 and 0.8, respectively. The cost per experimental case probably averaged about $4,000.[14]

PFF failed to report any significant difference in placement rates between experimental and control groups. There was even a curious although

13. This section on PFF appeared in William M. Epstein, *Welfare in America* (Madison: University of Wisconsin Press, 1997).

14. The authors have not evaluated the cost material. This is an estimate based on a phone discussion with Ms. Rzepnicki. The true cost differential is also difficult to estimate since no assessment was made of the costs of customary DCFS services during the experiment. Still, the amount spent on PFF experiment recalls the amounts spent on other intensive casework programs.

not statistically significant rise in placement rates among those who received family preservation services. The authors found

> little evidence that the program affects the risk of placement, subsequent maltreatment, or case closing and some evidence that the program may be related to short-term progress on case objectives. However, these results must be viewed in the context of considerable variation among sites and variations in outcomes that are due to characteristics of cases and the services provided to them. (Schuerman, Rzepnicki, and Littell 1994:188)

In addition, PFF seemed to produce a "net-widening effect" through which many families who were probably not at imminent risk of dissolution were accepted for family preservation care while their attentive case managers accounted for a dramatic increase in services for their caseloads. But once again, these services did not appear to ensure any improved outcomes. Especially by reinforcing two other large randomized studies, PFF seemed to dampen enthusiasm for IFPS. Yet its many methodological imperfections, especially taken in context of the mistargeting of the family preservation services, impede any conclusion.

In the first instance, the predictors of imminent risk were imprecise. As a result of this inability to predict placement as well as the experiment's difficulty in implementing randomization, PFF's family preservation services appear to have been mistargeted. In other words, family preservation was not fairly tested on its intended target group. Yet even while perceiving this problem early in the evaluative process, the researchers refused to abort the experiment.

Second, the experiment bypassed randomization for 24 percent of its subjects: 7 percent usually due to court orders and 16 percent at the discretion of caseworkers. While none of these cases (that did in fact receive the family preservation services) were included in the analyses, their exclusion compromises the representativeness of the samples. Indeed, these exclusions may account in large part for the poorly targeted samples. Moreover, the fact that these exclusions did no better than any other group raises the troubling possibility that family preservation, acknowledged as "intrusive," may exacerbate family problems.

Third, the study is marred by many measurement problems. PFF's outcome instruments never demonstrated acceptable levels of reliability. Indeed, the authors report that "evaluations of family preservation will continue to make use of measures of uncertain reliability, validity, and sensitivity" (Schuerman, Rzepnicki, and Littell 1994:212–13). Further, methods to gather data varied between the experimental and control groups. Moreover, the interviews with the experimental families were conducted by different groups of interviewers, presumably with different interviewing skills; the earlier interviewers were relatively inexperienced and untrained while the later interviews were conducted by professionals. In this way the outcomes of the interventions may reflect the different attitudes and experiences of the interviewers more than actual changes in target families.

Fourth, the treatment integrity (i.e., specification of the stimulus, definition of the intervention) of the family preservation intervention is suspect. PFF failed to independently check the receipt of services, relying on the reports of workers to measure the amounts and kinds of services.

Fifth, neither interviewers nor subjects were blind to their assignment.

Sixth, the fundamental outcome measure of the experiment, placement rates, may have been an inappropriate measure of the impact of the services. It may also have been an artifact of the experiment, where the intense surveillance of the experimental condition temporarily suppressed the actual family behaviors leading to placement while the superficial surveillance of the control condition failed to pick up abuses.

Finally, PFF faces a debilitating demonstration problem in which the laboratory of its service experiment enjoyed unusual worker motivations, intense surveillance by researchers, and creamed clients. Its experience may be unrepresentative of live service conditions, actual clients, or prevailing worker behaviors.

In the end, PFF is an unreliable study whose outcomes are at best indeterminate. Yet the authors pushed on to general recommendations about the American child welfare system that appear compatible with contemporary political tastes:

> The expansion of the purview of the child welfare system that has occurred in the last few decades should be stopped and reversed. This requires that lines be carefully drawn between our aspirations and what can be reasonably expected.... The state cannot accept responsibility for the optimal development of all children. Nor should it even endeavor to assure the "well-being" of all children given the impossibility of achieving that goal, even if well-being could be adequately defined and measured.... Emotional harms can, of course, have serious effects on the child, on the development of services to help parents better relate to their children. But these services should be voluntary, outside the abuse and neglect response system. (Schuerman, Rzepnicki, and Littell 1994:245)

However, the research neither established "reasonable expectations" nor in any way measured the desirability of state action or the state role per se. The authors offer triage and targeting efficiency, which may be near impossibilities, by way of arguing for a limited state role, apparently dropping out of their recommendations a broader concern for the seemingly entrenched problems of American poverty and institutional neglect.

Nevertheless, the authority for this partisan statement is not drawn from the research.

In light of the very minimal interventions of family preservation—its intensity is apparent only in relation to the neglect of customary care—PFF established little more, if even this much, than the probability that prior institutional and social deprivation exceeds the corrective capacities of intensive casework. The personal service approach to social problems may simply be inadequate to compensate for the structural problems and growing institutional inequalities of American life. The failure of family preservation services suggests that case management even under optimal conditions, when a variety of superficial treatment services are available for referral (which is not the common experience), may still be ineffective. Even if better funded, improved, and marginally intensified, personal social services may still be inadequate to compensate for the deep deprivations of the society.

More than most other evaluations of personal social services, PFF approximated rigorous research. The authors of PFF were unusually forthcoming in defining their methodological problems but this clarity by itself does not shift the burden of proof from their shoulders. As a result, the policy arena is deprived of credible information about the impacts of IFPS except perhaps for the general observation that, whoever the recipients and whatever their needs, intensive casework appears to be ineffective.

The poverty of the research on IFPS generally and the reaction to it is puzzling,

> given what the research has shown. Why is it that the child welfare establishment still enthusiastically advocates family preservation? Analogously, why do otherwise competent and surely intelligent persons publish . . . flawed data in order to advance the "family preservation" movement? Are we witnessing yet another triumph of faith over data? (Rossi 1994:464)

Rather than the quaint and aesthetic magic of faith, the triumph of political convenience over the needs of marginal social groups—notably poor children in need—may explain the professional compromises of the researchers. Family preservation programs are symbols that promote a broader ideology of parsimony. Children, and particularly dependent children, lose; winners include taxpayers, fiscal and social conservatives, social workers, and the growing number of low-expenditure liberals who have shifted the center of social policy in the United States. Flooding the landscape of contemporary American politics, these factions drown any dissent from the small number who see wisdom in higher taxes for a much larger public responsibility.

Fairy Dust and Cloth Poppies

Reunification strategies, family preservation programs, and other permanency planning initiatives, while prominent fixtures of the contemporary child welfare system, are only a few of the more successful instances of America's ingenuity at self-deception. Yet the inadequacies of child welfare programs periodically overwhelm the passionate blindness of adherents and their frail testimonials to efficacy. When it becomes apparent that child welfare services fail as substitutes for families, they also fail as convincing expressions of social concern. At these times, the human service research and development industry is challenged to fill holes in the public philosophy with ever new programmatic inspirations. By bending the practice of science, the industry typically produces symbols of charitability that have failed just as routinely as substantive, effective care.

> [The] style is not neoliberalism or neoconservatism, whatever those terms mean. It is something different, a kind of Government Lite. We want to improve conditions in depressed urban areas, so we show our good intentions by sprinkling a handful of federal fairy dust over them. (Menand 1997b:4)

Thus Menand rebukes Clinton for his cynical participation in the myth of social efficiency. Yet the same strategy has been an enduring and characteristic structure of American social dialectics. Hopeful leads—the sacraments of human service research—create a perennial optimism that tranquilizes the politics of human services by making need less visible. The wonderment lies in the ever-renewable American faith that simple, superficial, compatible, and inexpensive solutions will resolve its social dilemmas. Rather than weakening allegiances, the consistency of historical failure increases the culture's superstitious commitment to a vital lie—Joseph's prophecy and the horseplayer's fatal logic that a string of losers foretells a string of winners.

The human services' consideration of their efficacy has been structured around systematic summations of the primary outcome studies. In social work, these reviews gathered intensity with the publication of four critical works which nearly exhausted the field's critical tradition: Wootton's (1959) magisterial book, Segal's (1972) essay, Wood's (1978) analysis, and particularly Fischer's (1973b) bleak study. Taken together, these few reviews identified only a handful of outcome evaluations that reached even a minimal threshold of methodological credibility. Fischer concluded that American social work did not appear to be effective and that its scholarship was very thin, containing only eleven controlled evaluations of its effectiveness during a forty-year period. Moreover, Fischer hinted that social work services may be harmful: "In slightly under 50 percent of [Fischer's eleven] studies clients receiving services in the experimental group were shown either to deteriorate to a greater degree than clients in the control group or to demonstrate improved functioning at a lesser rate than control subjects" (1973b:15–16).

Subsequent reviews repaired the damage of doubt, reporting that professional social work was becoming truly effective and that its scholarship was achieving evaluative sophistication. Even Fischer was able to declare, less than a decade after ridiculing the field as Casey at the bat (Fischer 1973a), that a scientific revolution had taken place in social work (Fischer 1981). This declaration of a Kuhnian paradigm shift was made on the basis of "material presented at social work conferences, from the literature and from less concrete sources of evidence such as the new 'spirit' or 'world view' that seems to be emerging among many social workers," the use of behavioral interventions, and notably the adaption of single-subject research designs for program evaluation (1981:199).

Reid and Hanrahan (1982) followed along with a review that found "grounds for optimism." Taking his cue, Rubin (1985) shortly found "more grounds for optimism." Thomlison (1984) reassured the field that "something works." Sheldon (1986) added his support from Britain. Salutations were called in from other fields, notably clinical psychology, through meta-analyses (in particular, Smith, Glass, and Miller 1980), box-score reviews (Luborsky, Singer, and Luborsky 1975), and critical analyses (Lambert et al. 1986).[15] Criminology closed forces (Andrews et al. 1990) to refute its own skeptics (e.g., Martinson 1974). Since the 1970s, the end of the brief modern period of skepticism in the human services, the summary literature has been steadily becoming more confident and positive, stretching into many fields outside social work and providing consistent testimony for the programmatic feasibility of conservative social policy.[16]

However, the summary reviews both before and after Fischer's Disney-like contrivance of a scholarly revolution are deeply flawed, principally because they misinterpret and misreport the primary research. The base of studies, especially when viewed through a scientific lens, has been both less credible than the authors claim and also far less positive.[17] Social efficiency has triumphed over generosity on just about every battlefront of social

15. Meta-analysis is a technique to compare disparate studies by computing "effect sizes" for each of them. An effect size compares the outcomes (usually the percentage of patients who benefited from the intervention and the degree of their change) of experimental group patients with control group patients.

16. In particular, the personal service strategy of the 1996 welfare reform is endorsed widely through the social service literature per se as well as in the scholarship of the social sciences, notably including economics. See Epstein (1997) for an extended discussion of social science's role in public welfare, the 1996 reforms, and social services.

17. This argument is detailed by Epstein (1993, 1995).

problems. Social work's growing ebullience, as though it had been drinking the whiskey of success since 1973, has been topped off with Gorey's (1996) meta-analysis of outcome studies.

Gorey identified fully eighty-eight outcome studies that appeared between 1990 and 1994 in his base of thirteen "prestigious," peer-reviewed journals.[18] He seemed disappointed in the proportion of investigations of the field's effectiveness (one in eight) and the small number that were amenable to his quantification procedures. Still, the eighty-eight outcome studies that he analyzed represent more than four times the number found by Wood (1978) and eight times the number found by Fischer (1973b), who covered a much longer period of time. In a similar meta-analysis, Videka-Sherman (1988) identified only sixty-one relevant outcome studies over the nineteen years since 1965. Therefore, if Gorey's procedures are accurate, it would appear that social work's attention to its effectiveness is increasing dramatically.

Gorey concluded in corroboration of Videka-Sherman (1988) that "more than three-quarters of clients participating in [a social work] intervention do better than the average client who does not" (1996:124). Unfortunately, neither the research nor Gorey's procedures sustain this conclusion while the appearance of increasing scholarly attention to outcomes is illusory. Gorey included in his analysis any study reported in his base of journals that allowed him to compute an effect size. That is, he accepted any published research that included standard deviations and means and a design that included any sort of comparison group. Statistical significance was pointedly rejected in deference to clinical value, an amorphous notion that clinical practice somehow excuses the practitioner from rigorous tests of interventions. In direct defiance of standard scientific practice, the magnitude *alone* of the difference, unadjusted by the size of the samples, between the experimental group and the comparison group is taken to confer a special standing on the research. "Most social workers want more information about the magnitude of the intervention's effects or its effect size, which is more directly related to its clinical or policy significance . . . and more useful for grappling with cost–benefit concerns" (Gorey 1996:120). However, what clinicians want is not the same as what is useful for the ser-

18. He largely defined prestigious journals as those that accepted fewer than 50 percent of submitted articles. However, apart from the *Social Service Review* and possibly *Children and Youth Services Review,* it might more appropriately be argued that prestige within social work confers no standing in the general intellectual or social science community. Indeed, any high-quality research would more likely be published in the prestigious journals of the core social science disciplines. Without going on to bleed over methodology and meaning, Gorey could have cut to the chase: publication in a social work journal can customarily be taken as a sign that the research is defective.

vice recipient. Preliminary, small-sample, dubiously derived findings that are large may trigger greater interest in more rigorous testing. Yet by themselves, they are definitely not credible, let alone adequate, proofs. Until clinically interesting findings pass through the gauntlet of careful random controlled trials, they have not been sufficiently tested for their effects. To rush preliminary findings past definitive trials sacrifices the service recipient to professional convenience.

Moreover, Gorey failed to assess the general credibility of the primary research equating the findings from small convenience samples with large-sample objective trials. The reliability and validity of measures, the incorporation of protections against research bias, notably blinding, random selection and random assignment, the length of the follow-up period, the use of placebo controls, and so forth, are simply ignored in Gorey's single-minded march to professionally compatible conclusions.[19] Moreover, had Gorey adjusted the final effect size by subtracting a probable placebo effect, the percentage of clients helped might well be reduced by two-thirds.[20]

Gorey's failure to attend to the credibility of the base of research is particularly troublesome in light of his own earlier evidence for a strong institutional bias in the research. Cryns, Gorey, and Brice (1989) found that "the average effect reported by researchers affiliated with the institutions being evaluated was twice as large as the estimated effect based on external evaluations" (Gorey 1996:120).

Additionally, the base of primary research is customarily marred by numerous research flaws that invalidate its findings. Placebo effects have customarily accounted for two-thirds of the positive findings; biased and reactive measures, biased sampling, and so forth, probably account for the rest of the positive reports and perhaps for even a bit more. As a consequence, the possibility of routine deterioration as an outcome of service is a live possibility. In short, Gorey (1996) testifies less to the field's rational

19. Even Smith, Glass, and Miller (1980) gave considerable attention to the methodological quality of their base of studies. Unfortunately, this seminal meta-analysis, which has become a citation classic of psychotherapy's conceit, is irretrievably flawed (see Epstein 1984a, b). Moreover, their attention to method produced only a pompous excuse on grounds of subjectivity to reject rigorous inclusion criteria, " 'textbook' standards; these methodological rules, learned as dicta in graduate school and regarded as the touchstone of publishable articles in prestigious journals, were applied arbitrarily; for example, note again Rachman's high-handed dismissal on methodological grounds of study after study of psychotherapy outcome" (Smith, Glass, and Miller 1980:38).

20. The studies in Smith, Glass, and Miller (1980) allowed for this estimate; the studies in Gorey do not. A placebo effect is created by the patient's belief that he or she is being helped and should be distinguished from true planned therapeutic effects—the value added by trained therapists. The value of professional assistance is diminished to the extent that cure, prevention, and rehabilitation are engendered by nonprofessional conditions such as placebo care.

abilities and more to its bulk-cargo empiricism, the substitution of volume for substance, in appreciation of the process by which an undisciplined literature distorts science to fabricate its own social value.

The cloth poppies of philanthropy—therapeutic foster care, psychotherapy, and many other social service interventions that pursue cure, prevention, and rehabilitation—rattle off the imaginative production lines of child welfare research and development. Many fade out of consciousness as their star quality falters. Others pass the test of time with a charismatic draw on popular enthusiasm. Yet the effectiveness of child welfare services and social services generally has not enjoyed rational support—credible tests of their ability to address the problems that justify the services in the first place. The production functions of child welfare services—improved outcomes for children—are illusory. Their ceremonial roles in making the problems of child welfare invisible preside over social welfare dialectics.

False reports of success hide social need. If social problems are under control, then there is no reason to attend to them. The public's obvious desire to dismiss claims on the public treasury is facilitated by reassurances that children are being adequately cared for. Knitzer's (1982) happy listing of effective child welfare services, the two demonstrations (NOVA and MAPP) fueling GAO's (1989) optimism that an adequate supply of foster parents can be recruited, the treatment foster care crusade, and Daro's National Clinical Evaluation Study (1988) (NCES) are prominent instances of how spurious comfort is created by deceptive research.[21]

Knitzer (1982) on behalf of the Children's Defense Fund provides profiles of fifteen mental health programs for troubled children that she insists are effective: the Primary Prevention Program, the Regional Intervention Program (RIP), Project Enlightenment, the Positive Education Program, the Rose School, the Adolescent Day Treatment Center (ADTC), the Community-Based Intensive Treatment Program, the North Shore Children's Law Project, the Family Advocacy Council, Homebuilders, the Child Advocacy Treatment Team, the Children, Youth, and Family Services Program, Parent and Child Education Family Centers, the Cambridge and Somerville Program for Alcoholism Research (CASPAR), and Parents Supporting Parents. All of the programs offer a relatively inexpensive array of counseling and psychotherapeutic services. Knitzer boldly claims that "taken together, these programs affirm the legitimacy, value, and cost effectiveness of mental health services for children and adolescents" (1982:17).

21. Even this listing is easily extended with many additional but even more poorly evaluated programs that are still candidates for acceptance as customary child welfare services, for example, Chamberlain, Moreland, and Reid (1992); Cornish and Nelson (1991); *Journal of the American Medical Association* (1997); Kennedy and Keeney (1987); Resnick and Burt (1996); Schaeffer et al. (1981); and Simms (1989).

Yet she goes on to provide mailing addresses to the organizations boosting these interventions more frequently than specific citations to the evidence for their efficacy.

In the end, none of Knitzer's claims for positive outcomes are demonstrated; indeed, the reports of program effectiveness frequently do not exist or appear as smoke signals in the most suspect of gray publications— the ephemeral outlets of a fugitive literature.[22]

The few existing evaluations of Knitzer's fifteen projects report ambiguous outcomes at best; they are methodologically unsound; they are often the essays of true believers. As discussed previously, Homebuilders as well as family preservation generally have not demonstrated their effectiveness. Davis et al. (1985) evaluated CASPAR with only a questionnaire that tested whether children had absorbed information about alcoholism. In a similar way, the other evaluations of CASPAR (Brown and Sunshine 1982; DiCicco et al. 1984; and DiCicco, Davis, and Orenstein 1984) addressed only its processes, not its outcomes, making brave and convenient assumptions that the acquisition of information is tantamount to its use. The important outcome, unevaluated for CASPAR, is a reduced probability of later problems, including alcoholism, among children of alcoholics.

The literature offers only a single case study of "an aggressive emotionally disturbed pre-adolescent boy" to evaluate the Rose School (Levison 1982) and a single qualitative essay in support of the value of the Family Advocacy Council. Linnihan (1977) does not evaluate the effectiveness of ADTC, but only describes the program. Knitzer concedes that "although no comprehensive study has been made of [ADTC's] effectiveness, staff believe institutional care has been prevented in at least half the cases"—quite a comedown for evidence of positive outcomes (Knitzer 1982: 26).

Of Knitzer's fifteen programs, RIP seems to have received the greatest attention in the literature (Fields 1975; Fitzgerald and Fischer 1987; Fitzgerald and Karnes 1987; Hester 1977; Hester and Hendrickson 1977; Parrish and Hester 1980; Regional Intervention Program 1976; Strain et al. 1982; Timm and Rule 1981). However, only three actual studies (contained in four of these publications) report outcomes. The cost–benefit value of the project was assessed on only ten unrepresentative subjects and reported secondhand without any detailed description of methods or measures (Hester 1977; Regional Intervention Program 1976). A second study incorporated a single subject design on only three patients with the therapist serving as the evaluator (Hester and Hendrickson 1977). Finally,

22. Knitzer fails to provide references to any evidence for the effectiveness of nine of these fifteen programs. Furthermore, the current PyschLit and Social Science Indexes contain no reference to, let alone an evaluation of, six of these nine programs.

Strain et al. (1982) conducted a nonrandom follow-up evaluation of forty successfully treated children, finding that success persisted. However, the methodologically limited research could not assess the severity of the children's initial problems, the amount of the agency's overall success with its service recipients, or the degree to which initial treatment was actually related to the final successful outcomes. In short, credible evaluations of RIP and of Knitzer's fourteen other bulletins of success from the human services' frontlines have still to take place. Yet the programs seem to sustain devoted staffs and supportive constituencies.

GAO (1989) relies on two programs—NOVA and MAPP—to justify the conclusions that more foster parents can be recruited and that their quality can be improved through mandatory training. However, GAO's evidence does not sustain its recommendations. Pasztor (1985) simply lauds NOVA's training methods. The evaluation by Simon and Simon (1982)— the director of the NOVA program and a graduate assistant—reported that within the one-year period after mandatory foster parent training, the trained group was more productive than the untrained group, and the district actually recruited more foster parents. However, the research does not address the quality of care provided by foster parents, that is, the actual benefit to the foster children.

Moreover, alternative explanations for the outcomes are not addressed, the possibilities: that recruitment took advantage of a backlog of volunteers that was exhausted after the one-year follow-up period; that greater generic attention to foster parents and recruitment produced favorable outcomes; or that greater attention by caseworkers to experimental group subjects produced the positive outcomes.

The placement of foster children in the two groups does not appear to have been random. Children placed with trained foster parents seem to have been more difficult and troubled than those placed with untrained parents; however, they were also much better known to the caseworkers and could either have been creamed for success or provided with a greater amount of supportive care. Finally, the trained experimental group and untrained control were not formed through random assignment and therefore it is impossible to attribute the outcomes to training rather than to screening. In any jurisdiction it is possible to identify a small number of highly motivated and skilled foster parents. However, the NOVA research failed to address the central question of whether it is possible to convert the common foster care volunteer into a quality foster parent through minimal training. The inexpensive NOVA model has spread to many other jurisdictions, but it is still not apparent that it can make any enduring contribution to the quality of foster care.

The MAPP experience is apparently buried at irretrievable depths in the fugitive literature (items that appeared five times in a publicity serial of the Massachusetts Department of Social Services in 1987 and 1988 plus unavailable items from an obscure research institute).[23] Presumably, if MAPP's positive outcomes could be sustained even on the margins of credulity the documentation would surely have surfaced in at least one of the field's many journals. In the end, then, a prominent government agency is hiding a serious social problem—the persistent if not growing difficulty of finding acceptable surrogate parents—beneath an unwise enthusiasm for an inexpensive and simplistic program. It is most likely that foster parent training has very little to offer while foster parent screening has much to say for itself. Unfortunately, not enough skilled people are willing to become foster parents and the people's government refuses to announce this problem with candor.

Treatment foster care (TFC) is usually temporary, psychotherapeutic treatment that is often provided through a congregate, residential foster care program. Galaway, Hudson, and Nutter (1995) screened the literature for "systematic" evaluations of TFC's effectiveness. They identified only seven programs that met their inclusion criteria. Reporting that the research suffered from many methodological problems, they danced around the issue of effectiveness but in the end they salvaged hope, piecing together a series of positive conclusions about disposition, cost, program completion, and client change that they felt justified a definitive "randomized experiment" to test the effectiveness of TFC.

Yet their base of research is "systematic" in only the broadest sense, failing to include representative or routinely large samples, comparable control groups (let alone randomly created controls or placebos, with a few studies including no comparison group at all), reliable measures, reliable measurement procedures (notably multiple blinding), explicit descriptions of the interventions, assurance of treatment integrity, and so forth. Even within the debased scholarship of child welfare, these studies are notable for their weakness (Almeida, Hawkins, Meadowcroft, and Luster 1989; Bogart 1988; Chamberlain, 1988, 1990; Colton 1988, 1990; Fanshel, Finch, and Grundy 1989, 1990; Hazel 1981, 1990; Larson and Allison 1977; Larson, Allison, and Johnston 1978; Levin, Rubinstein, and Streiner 1976; Rubenstein, Amentrout, Levin, and Herald 1978; Smith 1986; Yelloly 1979). Researches subsequent to Galaway, Hudson, and Nutter (1995) have ignored their recommendations and continue to discover the virtues of TFC in weak research (Evans et al. 1994; Ray and

23. Yet more ludicrous, the Child Welfare Institute in Atlanta will release *Model Approach to Partnerships in Parenting for Foster Parents and Adoptive Parents* only to those licensed to teach the MAPP program. The report is apparently a description and evaluation of MAPP and listed among the references in the GAO report.

Horner 1990; Staff and Fein 1995). Still, a timid voice of doubt concludes that "research findings from field-based studies of psychotherapy indicate weak (at best) results of psychotherapy as an intervention as currently practiced in community-based clinics" (Kutash and Rivera 1995:468). Indeed, there is no credible evidence that any psychotherapeutic intervention has been successful, let alone temporary and shallow programs for very troubled youth (Epstein 1995), and little puzzle that TFC programs have avoided credible outcome evaluation for years.

Initiated by the federal government's National Center for Child Abuse and Neglect (NCCAN), the often referenced Daro project—*Evaluation of the Clinical Demonstrations of the Treatment of Child Abuse and Neglect*—purports to show that psychotherapeutic interventions can be successful in handling either the perpetrators or the victims of child abuse (Berkeley Planning Associates 1982; Daro 1988). During three and one-half years, the project studied four types of child maltreatment: physical abuse, physical neglect, sexual abuse, and emotional maltreatment. Daro's findings were based on nineteen specially funded research demonstrations by NCCAN as well as an extensive reanalysis of "more than 100 research studies and program evaluations conducted over the past 20 years" (Daro 1988:4).

> All of the nineteen demonstrations provided a full array of therapeutic as well as nontherapeutic services to their clients. Parenting education classes, assistance in securing welfare benefits and health care services, recreational activities to reduce social isolation, homemaker services, and vocational and job training assistance were provided by these projects along with at least one therapeutic service modality. (Daro 1988:112)

The project reports great success, although some groups benefited more than others. "For example, 64% of the adults primarily involved in sexual abuse were judged by their clinicians to be unlikely to maltreat their children further, an assessment given to only 30% of the adults primarily involved in child neglect" (Daro 1988:103). This success with sexual abusers increased to over 70 percent in projects specifically designed for them.

The outcomes with victims were even more impressive, especially considering their uniform adoption of "a family treatment focus rather than an individual one" (Daro 1988:112).

> All told, over 1,600 children and adolescents were provided a wide range of direct services including individual therapy, group counseling, therapeutic day care, speech and physical therapy, and medical care. This rich array of services correlated with improved functioning for children and adolescents who had experienced a variety of abusive and neglectful be-

haviors. . . . Over 70% of the young children and adolescents served by the eight projects focusing specifically on these client populations demonstrated gains across all functional areas during treatment. (Daro 1988:113)

These extraordinary successes, providing a boost to beleaguered psychotherapy, led Daro to come to emphatic and "heartening" conclusions: "greater clarity in understanding" treatment needs, "expanded intervention models," "improved client outcomes," and "notable success in initially reducing the risk for future maltreatment among families involved in sexual abuse" (1988:121).

Unfortunately, none of these conclusions hold water and the manifest biases and limitations of the research design raise questions again about the motives of the federal government in funding this research. The research employed no comparison group of any sort, let alone a randomized, placebo control. Moreover, all the assessments of improvement were made by the therapists, frequently relying on the self-report of their clients (Berkeley Planning Associates 1982).[24] It is simply foolhardy to expect therapists to provide independent and accurate assessments of their own success. The common practice for evaluating psychotherapeutic outcomes avoided this pitfall of research well before the Daro project (Smith, Glass, and Miller 1980). Furthermore, the Daro project relied on the self-report of the clients, who at a minimum were under stern scrutiny for violating social taboos; they would be highly unlikely to confess their continuing sins. The fact that the government endorsed these procedures raises the issue of its complicity in creating comforting evidence, indeed propaganda, for the sufficiency of the society's desultory responses to serious behavioral problems including prevalent and offensive crimes.

Society's Neglect of Public Child Welfare

The applied social sciences and all of their attendant core academic disciplines that together constitute the field of child welfare take a chest-feather pride in what they know. In truth, "what we know" is a gnomic conceit of

24. Moreover, the research is not readily available, seemingly lost in the gray literature. Daro (1988) lists nine study reports in her appendix A (234). None are listed in the Library of Congress catalog. None seem to be available from the source (NCCAN). Only one (volume 2, *The Exploration of Client Characteristics, Services and Outcomes*) was provided by the authors, Berkeley Planning Associates. This is not surprising in consideration of the stunning weaknesses, even within a weak literature, of the whole investigative effort. The *Evaluation of the Clinical Demonstrations of the Treatment of Child Abuse and Neglect* is neither responsible social science nor a tribute to the dispassionate search for evidence of program outcomes by a democratic and responsive government.

professionalism. The field does not know the rudiments of its operations or its outcomes and it lacks the self-discipline or largeness of character to find out. It spends its scarce resources to create a series of factional studies for its own ideological and political advantage, furthering both the fiction that it knows what to do and that its preferences are in the interests of maltreated children. In the most fundamental way, the field has not bothered to find out what maltreated children need and how those needs can be met.

A critical review of child welfare programs cannot sustain any buoyant view of their efficacy. The experiments, analyses, and demonstrations that led to the passage of the Act of 1980, as well as the evaluations of the programs that the act supported, are not believable. Indeed, for at least the contemporary period of the past forty years, the feebleness and failure of these programs and the evaluative blindness of the literature suggest that generous interventions may be needed either to protect children or to restore them to appropriate functioning.

It is doubtful that the scholarly community that has created these misleading parables of public kindness exercises a responsible stewardship of children in need: truth would serve them better than the ambitions of their Boswells. If the American public is to protect itself from feral children who grow into problematic adults, then the child welfare system must do more than shepherd the abused, neglected, and troubled to abandonment at the age of eighteen or to take palpable risks with their safety in abusive foster homes, improbable adoptions, and premature reunifications with their birth parents.

The child welfare system may have changed little over the past decades except that it now handles many more children. Total, lifetime duration in care may still be very long. It is not clear whether the child welfare reforms of the past twenty-five years are having any influence; the programs that they inspired are poorly evaluated, indeterminate, and probably ineffective. There remain strong suspicions that even in spite of the formal changes the system is still terribly inadequate.

The inadequacy of the child welfare system may come down to the superficiality of its services, representing a pragmatic political consensus that solutions can be socially efficient. Whether providing concrete services, counseling, or a mix of the two, the interventions may well have uniformly failed. The theories that inspired the services are empty. The structural logic that endorses concrete services and the subcultural logic of counseling both assume that the deprivations they address are minor and that the causes of personal dysfunction have been identified by the social sciences. Unfortunately, a few hours of concrete assistance and injunctions to become personally responsible will not repair the ravages of American poverty, the awful effects of becrazed parents on their children, sinister neighborhood influences, or oppositional subcultures. However, the incessant testimonials of the research for the success of superficial care and the promise of each generation of hopeful leads make invisible and inaudible the gravity of social conditions.

Superficiality together with the conservative preference for a barbaric neglect has justified a system based on less eligibility, the notion that children in public care should be provided for at the least eligible level—just a stroke off of poverty and degradation. In this way, the failure of child welfare services is also the profound expression of a public philosophy of pernicious liberalism belaboring the fiction that socially efficient services are also effective in addressing serious social deprivations.

Adequate child welfare services require a bolstering, ennobling theory and a supportive public. At a minimum children without parents need services that offer effective surrogate family experiences. Children deprived of nurturing families lack the critical socialization experiences necessary to grow into complete adults and responsible citizens. The heart of the problem in child welfare services lies with a refusal to come to grips with the nature of their needs for substitute families.

4
Pernicious Liberalism
and Painted Birds

Building dysfunctional personalities around enormous anger, Natalie and Adam live everywhere in the public child welfare system. Extended battering and maltreatment by natural parents, by caretakers, and by their own peers in a ferocious subculture of youth have routinely deprived children in public care of both psychic ease and a sense of their own worth. Their parents' lessons in humiliation, repeated in foster homes with an unintended humor as parody of family tradition, have taught self-contempt. The children rage at the injustice of it, spewing oblivious hatred, especially at adults in positions of authority. The most unfortunate of these children retreat from continuous insults to remote points of safety, in time turning up in prison, on wards for psychotics, or drugged into plastic obedience.

Like all children, foster children lack the dispassion and strength to wall off the judgments of their parents. Although often aware of their parents' emotional deformities, they still torment themselves with their parents' inescapable scorn. The violation of personal security and privacy is perhaps the worst abuse they suffer, even worse than the beatings and the sexual exploitation from which they eventually escape.

Foster children consume themselves in a haggard pursuit of self-respect—to become a member of a family and to be endowed with value and love—that destroys the calm necessary to complete the important tasks in preparation for adulthood, notably education. They become lost in adolescence, characteristically behind in school, without self-discipline or important socialization skills, and isolated from simple human relations by their hostilities and embedded distrust.

The society achieves its pious conceits by assuring through its system of public neglect that many of the children become the devils of their parents' lessons. The children are straitjacketed into regimented child care programs, and as soon as they are emancipated from legal control, usually at eighteen years of age, they explode into orgies of self-indulgence. The violence and humiliations they suffered are visited back, indiscriminately in the most extreme cases, with mindless violence and disregard for the consequences of their rebellions even to themselves. The children's blunt deficiencies, tragically confirming their fears of unworthiness, do not vindicate their parents' judgments. Rather than a justification of the system's harshness, their flaws are scheduled by what they have gone through.

Nevertheless, foster children must get past their bad times, their anger, and their own desires for vengeance and violence if they are to become functioning adults and responsible citizens. Understanding their parents as imperfect if not actually failed human beings—a tortuous task for a youth, let alone a mature adult—is part of the process. The fact that these teens are not loved by their own parents or by their many custodians does not mean that they are unlovable and unworthy. Yet the self-denigration and rage that define the personality cores of many foster children are the undomesticated legacies of the public child welfare system and the society's refusal to provide asylum for youth without political influence. Children in public care truly test the nation's philanthropic impulses.

The public child welfare system routinely fails to socialize children, largely because it refuses to offer either appropriate surrogates for the family or appropriate shortcuts to socialization in lieu of surrogates. Nevertheless, shortcuts to socialization, tried repeatedly throughout the sorry program history of public child welfare, may not be possible. Only the rarest congregate foster care program and only a minority of foster families deliver the basic assurances of physical security along with intellectual stimulation and a unique bond of affection with at least one responsible adult.

Congregate programs and family foster care, notably kinship care, frequently continue the abuse and neglect of natural parents. Adoptions of older children often falter and the true disruption rate is very likely far in excess of the reported 20 percent. Moreover, diversion programs (preservation, reunification, and the rest) have fared as badly as programs that provide more concrete services while early emancipation simply dresses up social indifference as programmatic wisdom. The system's programs—underfunded, short-term, insecure, and often all three—are miserable surrogates for the family.

Yet a true surrogate for the social institution of family must copy its substance as well as its form—all of the functions and expressions of family life and not just those that generate conformity and obedience. Since effective care has not been realized through a strategy of social efficiency, the child welfare system might profitably experiment with the widespread use of relatively permanent, well-funded, small congregate settings.

In the context of current care, Boys Town is unusual, even heroic. However, to socialize essentially feral children and to avoid continuing abuse, the child welfare system needs to improve on Boys Town, providing a greater amount of unregimented living and access to a greater range of intellectual, cultural, emotional, and social experiences. An adequate surrogate for the family should also offer more opportunities for self-expression while placing less emphasis on vocational preparation, giving each of its children permission to be at home and to stay in touch well past the age of eighteen. The bill for this kind of care is enormous; each place at Boys Town costs more than fifty thousand dollars per year.[1]

However, this level of funding and a thoroughgoing revitalization of the public child welfare system will probably not take place, especially while the private, philanthropic sector has long been unwilling to fund the gap between public budgets and needed care. Rather, the nation pursues social efficiency, not compassion, wisdom, or justice, while its intellectual expressions—in this case, the literature of children's services—surrender to the majoritarian preferences of the culture and not its beleaguered minorities' need for effective assistance. Without any consideration of merit or worthiness, the intellectual life of the field has suborned the rigors of objectivity and truth in justifying less public responsibility, even for America's most worthy citizens. Moral imperatives do not naturally mature into enforceable claims and the standing of children—presumably innocent and deserving—has not awakened public largesse.

Programs that might successfully address the needs of abandoned and maltreated children are apparently not politically feasible. Moreover, the needs of these children are simply one instance of a much larger concern with social adjustment and fairness in the United States. Indeed, it is very expensive to address the daunting problems of economic and cultural poverty along with the equally difficult problems of personal adjustment. Yet both need to be handled if the United States is to progress beyond its economic growth. This dilemma of social welfare—the political implausibility of possibly effective solutions—is given dramatic meaning by the very stratified economics of the United States. Not so strangely, those who are the quickest to recant goals of perfectibility are right on the line to foot that bill.

Social Efficiency and the Failure of Shortcuts

Socially efficient approaches to the problems of families have uniformly failed. The provision of psychotherapy and of modest levels of short-term

---

1. This estimate is based on Boys Town's figures for care in Las Vegas, Nevada, a relatively low-cost city. Comparable care in denser population centers is likely to be considerably more.

concrete services (either separately or together) have neither prevented placement nor reunited broken families. To the contrary, child welfare services often continue the abuses of natural placements. More generally, underfunded strategies of care, transmitting little more than the culture's pieties, have also failed to handle important social problem such as poverty, drug abuse, homelessness, educational deficiencies, mental and emotional problems, or criminal behavior.

The critical analysis of the outcome literature of public child welfare programs monotonously underscores four conclusions. First, the quality of the research is poor. Although child welfare may well be the oldest obligation of both public welfare and welfare scholarship, child welfare research appears to be the weakest area of investigation. Studies are methodologically porous, lagging decades behind the sophistication of the social sciences. Even acknowledging the public's unwillingness to provide sufficient research moneys, the evaluative studies of child welfare are marred by many unnecessary methodological pitfalls: the absence of controls or the use of inappropriate controls; unreliable and biased measures; inadequate follow-up periods; the failure to protect against researcher bias; the failure to ensure treatment integrity, that is, the failure to accurately describe interventions and to conform with research protocols; the reliance on inaccurate and distorted data such as administrative records; and so forth.

The research has failed to describe the conditions of the children before placement, in placement, or afterward, thus depriving them of even a minimal advocacy. This is the most profound indictment of the field's scholarship. At best the many studies quantify changes in dispositions—who and how many children went where—but they fail to evaluate both the actual quality of services against any standard of care and the effects of the programs on the children. The suspicion remains strong that placement decisions—frequently no more than automatic adjustments to public fervor for one style or another of socially efficient program—reflect pressures on agencies to save money rather than secure the health, safety, and welfare of maltreated children.

In short, the research is not scientifically credible. As a result, there is no adequate assessment of the quality of care or the determinants—the causes—of service outcomes. Without verified causal relations, the theories of intervention are naturally weak. Consequently, little rational authority exists either to defend current care or to recommend changes on grounds of effectiveness. The universe of discourse relative to child welfare is uniformly political.

Second, the evaluative studies routinely exaggerate the effectiveness of the programs. Indeed, the programs are customarily evaluated by those with the greatest stakes in their success: the program designers, the practitioners, and beholden investigators. Simple reinterpretations of the existing data often suggest that the programs are actually ineffective. The enthusiasm created by a decade of preparatory experiments for the Act of 1980 was unwarranted. Indeed, serious congressional scrutiny of those five studies, the best of the crop, would have halted any movement toward the act's measures. However, the nation's political process moves not toward rational but toward political ends, and the desire to contain costs while preserving comfortable social institutions limits any inclination to reform the system.

Third, only a relatively narrow range of program interventions has been studied. The nation has rarely experimented with generosity while it has customarily ignored its own neglect; the programs that are evaluated generally offer only superficial care.

Fourth, the consistent absence of rigorous research, the general refusal to evaluate the system, and the small public budgets for research suggest that there is no compelling political interest in the quality of the public child welfare system. Rather than providing advocacy and protection for children denied responsible parents, the society is largely content with the current system. Even periodic deaths of children in care have little effect on public budgets or programs.

It is difficult to conclude that child welfare researchers constitute a "community of the competent" that merits university standing (Haskell 1996). Moreover, the deficiencies of the child welfare research and more broadly the social sciences to create scientifically credible information are not innocent. The methodological pitfalls of the research appear to bolster professional conveniences. Its many distortions have generally dramatized the myths of governance—the fiction that socially efficient service programs are steps in the right direction, hopeful leads, as much as can be done, noble efforts, and humane, insightful beginnings. The tendentious research provides symbolic permission through the metaphors of service— public child welfare programs as effective if not actually epic triumphs— for the society to pursue its political interests. In this sense, the failure of science is also a failure of benevolence.

The literature is not simply dramatizing a point of etiquette in its distorted descriptions and evaluations of child welfare programs. Rather, the literature's myths facilitate the accommodation between social need and political preference—the reconciliation of social aspiration with the reality of power. American liberalism, envious of the popularity of conservatives, has embraced social efficiency. Parsimony in expenditures and a slavish respect for existing social institutions have induced the center, including the Democratic Party, to recant substantive reform in favor of procedural equality, if even this.

The Literature of Child Welfare and Pernicious Liberalism

By obscuring the inadequacies of existing programs and by grossly exaggerating the effectiveness of inexpensive experimental programs, the research advances a mock-progressive agenda that perniciously denies resources and social attention to those in need. Pernicious liberalism defies the principles of progressive liberalism, largely a structural theory of social causation that endorses the public claims of poorer populations. Structural social policies assume that problems can be avoided or handled by changing the conditions of living through substantive interventions. In this way, economic poverty and perhaps even cultural poverty are reduced by the provision of public works, income supports, and training and job preparation programs. Similarly, cultural poverty—emerging from severely deficient participation in the basic institutions of society—requires greater programmatic attention to families, communities, the employment market, schooling, health, and so forth.

Following this logic, dysfunctional families need more functional environments, perhaps entailing housing, jobs, and personal supervision. Delinquent children, those without families, and the maltreated and abandoned may require socialization in surrogate families, that is, environments that replicate the family in order to replicate its functions. In this way, structural theories tend to argue for greater equality of participation in the institutions of society in order to resolve social problems.

By contrast, conservative political thought in the United States assumes subcultural and characterological causes of social failure. Poverty is largely the result of oppositional subcultures that teach deviance, sloth, intemperance, and disrespect for education and authority. Personal problems, including substance abuse, violence, and emotional dysfunctions, are largely moral issues of personal choice. In both cases, the onus is on individuals to reform themselves. If society has any obligation at all, it is to provide incentives for self-reflection and opportunities for personal renewal. Psychotherapy, in spite of its mimicry of medicine's clinical science, is nested in personal theories of deviance; it has functioned as a secular inspiration for the epiphany of personal responsibility. If social failure is personal, then current distributions of social and economic rewards are largely just; the winners have earned their rewards.

However, both theories remain articles of faith—ideologies of causation and social desserts—since experimental verification of their tenets is neither morally nor practically feasible. The United States cannot be randomized to provide a control for state intervention. For this reason, economics and the other policy disciplines are not truly experimental sciences with the result that their assertions are necessarily uncertain and usually greatly so.

Moreover, structural and subcultural theories quickly become confounded. Longstanding structural inequalities may produce true subcultural adaptations. In this case, it may be necessary to impose sanctions for personal choices, especially when the sustaining structural factors are no longer present. Similarly, persistent subcultural preferences may entail different personal and economic outcomes even when there are no initial and telling structural differences; subcultural differences may facilitate structural differentiations of both caste and class.

Even while it is impossible to verify general theories of social causation, it frequently is possible to evaluate the social interventions that they imply, especially when those programs are conducted in clinical settings. Presumably, successful programs provide at least tentative support for their underlying theories. However, the academic community generally and the social sciences in particular have failed to conduct credible evaluations of social welfare programs. To the contrary, they have largely acquiesced in pernicious liberalism by failing to credibly test the principles of social efficiency through program evaluations. These professional lapses by the community of social scientists conveniently avoid political conflicts with those in power. Yet flaccid and evasive program evaluation facilitates the slide of social policy to the right by tolerating, if not actually creating, self-serving and inaccurate claims to program effectiveness while muffling the progressive voice.

Pernicious liberalism imposes the myth of social efficiency on public child welfare services as a series of programs (reunification, preservation, psychotherapy, foster care, congregate care, etc.) and propositions about the nature of the system (it simply needs a bit more attention; voluntary efforts and auspices are preferable to public programs; the business community's acumen is needed in child welfare agencies; foster care is not so bad; services are largely effective and humane). The production of these myths is probably the core function of academic social welfare.

At a minimum the causes of child abuse and neglect are indeterminate, a result of the porous social science research. The child welfare experiments, especially in consideration of their feeble interventions, achieved none of their goals: family restoration or preservation, protection of children, reduction of mental and emotional problems, reduction of poverty, and so forth. In a number of cases, notably in Nashville and in other diversion programs, it was likely that the public sector saved money at least for a short time but it was not apparent that the children benefited. Nevertheless, it is not clear that the experiments that reported more favorable dispositions did so without forcing children to remain in precarious homes.

Indeed, very few of the studies—Fanshel and Shinn (1978) is one of the few exceptions—ever bothered to measure the actual conditions of the children. Instead, they settled for frequency counts of dispositions as a proxy for quality under the a priori assumption that home care was preferable to placement. Moreover, the most credible evaluation of a child welfare program ever conducted—family preservation in Illinois (Schuerman, Rzepnicki, and Littell 1994)—offered concrete services as the core of its intervention and it seemed to fail. The conviction that the child welfare literature has consistently demonstrated that more concrete services lead to better dispositions is plausible only if the researchers' interpretations of their own data are accepted in isolation and ignorance of the pitfalls of their research.

It is as unreasonable to conclude that poverty is a result of deviant behavior as to assume the reverse. However, it is not unreasonable to conclude that whatever the assumptions of cause, the interventions that have been tried have failed. The statement of failure is important since it directs public attention to unresolved problems. By ignoring the reality of programmatic failure, tepid liberalism is remarkably similar to tepid conservatism in denying the enduring gravity of social problems and in supporting a pernicious liberalism. This widely popular political consensus, constructed from the tatters of contemporary social science, underpins the slide of social welfare policy away from public responsibility for individual failure. It repudiates a complex structuralism with the goal of greater cultural equality and accepts the inevitability of the minimal condescension of an inadequate social provision.

The consistent inability of the human services—notably child welfare services—to demonstrate the effectiveness of any of its weak interventions suggests that more intensive interventions are necessary to handle social problems. If anything, the literature has proven that human habits are mulishly impervious to trivial inducements and blandishments. The experiments that employed largely concrete interventions—the five studies that led up to the Act of 1980 as well as subsequent experiments and notably the Illinois evaluation of family preservation—produced no better results than those employing largely behavioral or psychotherapeutic care. At best, the outcomes of child welfare are indeterminate. More probably the programs are ineffective while suspicion recurs that they may even be harmful, especially since dispositions can be forced by bureaucratic fiat.

The possibility of harm in inadequately funded and dogmatically championed social welfare programs is far more prevalent (and insidious for being unacknowledged) than current social dialectics is willing to concede. Perhaps many of the programs were humanely conceived, although "so many of the well-intentioned interventions—public housing, for example, or urban renewal, or busing—have only worsened the situation"

(Rybczynski 1998:14). Then again, many social welfare programs, including the public child welfare system, seem sinister after persisting for many decades in the face of profound criticism without credible proof of their effectiveness. Some initiatives—charter schools, community policing, empowerment zones, behavioral treatment, family preservation and reunification, community foster care, and the like—are probably intended as little more than political diversion, the entertainments produced by an ever obliging cadre of professionals to sustain popular faith in welfare minimalism. Yet the misrepresentation of social welfare programs obscures the inadequacies of current society, cozening a pernicious liberalism that may exact a larger price than contemporary fiscal emergencies.

The Painted Bird

> The 1980s, which also seemed to overwhelm old values with new life-styles dedicated to cash and the flesh, had a [pernicious] impact. Now there is a reaction, into horrified and lachrymose questioning. Where is decency, or community feeling? Where, above all, is innocence? (Ascherson 1998:30)

Jerzy Kosinski answers timelessly in *The Painted Bird*. An innocent child is made to travel through one torment after another in rural Eastern Europe during World War II. He passes some days with a farmer, Lehk, who, frustrated and denied by his lover, catches a small bird and paints its wings. The bird flies back to its flock but the flock does not recognize it.

> The painted bird circled from one end of the flock to the other, vainly trying to convince its kin that it was one of them. But, dazzled by its brilliant colors, they flew around it unconvinced. The painted bird would be forced farther and farther away as it zealously tried to enter the ranks of the flock. We saw soon afterwards how one bird after another would peel off in a fierce attack. Shortly the many-hued shape lost its place in the sky and dropped to the ground. (Kosinski 1965:57)

Kosinski paints the child with the cruelties of Eastern Europe and in the end the innocent becomes as sadistic as Lehk. It need not be so.

Bibliography
Index

Bibliography

Albert, V. 1994. "Explaining Growth in the Number of Child Abuse and Neglect Reports and Growth in the Foster Care Caseload." In R. P. Barth, J. D. Berrick, and N. Gilbert (eds.), *Child Welfare Research Review*, vol. 1. New York: Columbia University Press.

Anderson, J. L., and B. Simonitch. 1981. Reactive depression in youths experiencing emancipation. *Child Welfare* 60(6):383–90.

Andrews, D. A., I. Zinger, R. D. Hoge, J. Bonta, P. Gendreau, and F. T. Cullen. 1990. Does correctional treatment work? A clinically relevant and psychologically informed meta-analysis. *Criminology* 28(3):419–29.

Ascherson, N. 1998. Lost. *New York Review of Books*. January 15, pp. 30–31.

Babcock, C. 1965a. Some psychodynamic factors in foster parenthood—part one. *Child Welfare* 44(9):485–93.

Babcock, C. 1965b. Some psychodynamic factors in foster parenthood—part two. *Child Welfare* 44(10):570–86.

Barth, R. P. 1988. Disruption in older child adoptions. *Public Welfare* 46(1):23–29.

Barth, R. P. 1990. On their own: The experiences of youth after foster care. *Child and Adolescent Social Work Journal* 7(5):419–40.

Barth, R. P. 1992. "Adoption." In P. J. Pecora, J. K. Whittaker, and A. N. Maluccio (eds.), *The Child Welfare Challenge: Policy, Practice, and Research*. New York: Aldine de Gruyter.

Barth, R. P., J. D. Berrick, M. Courtney, and V. Albert. 1994. *From Child Abuse to Permanency Planning: Child Welfare Services Pathways and Placements*. New York: Aldine de Gruyter.

Barth, R. P., J. D. Berrick, and N. Gilbert (eds.). 1994. *Child Welfare Research Review*, vol. 1. New York: Columbia University Press.

Barth, R. P., and M. Berry. 1988. *Adoption and Disruption: Rates, Risks, and Responses*. New York: Aldine de Gruyter.

Barth, R. P., and M. Berry. 1994. "Implication of Research on the Welfare of Children under Permanency Planning." In R. P. Barth, J. D. Berrick, and N. Gilbert (eds.), *Child Welfare Research Review*, vol. 1. New York: Columbia University Press.

Benedict, M. I., and R. B. White. 1991. Factors associated with foster care length of care. *Child Welfare* 70(1):45–58.

Benedict, M. I., R. B. White, and R. Stallings. 1987. Race and length of stay in foster care. *Social Work Research and Abstracts* 23(4):23–26.

Berrick, J. D., R. Barth, and N. Gilbert. 1997. *Child Welfare Research Review*, vol. 2. New York: Columbia University Press.

Berrick, J. D., M. E. Courtney, and R. P. Barth. 1993. Specialized foster care and group home care: Similarities and differences in the characteristics of children in care. *Children and Youth Services Review* 15:453–75.

Besharov, D. J. 1985. Doing something about child abuse: The need to narrow the grounds for state intervention. *Harvard Journal of Law and Public Policy* 8:539–89.

Block, N. M., and A. S. Libowitz. 1983. *Recidivism in Foster Care*. New York: Child Welfare League of America.

Bloom, H. 1992. *The American Religion*. New York: Simon and Schuster.

Bohman, M., and S. Sigvardsson. 1990. "Outcomes in Adoption: Lessons from Longitudinal Studies." In D. Brodzinsky and M. Schechter (eds.), *The Psychology of Adoption*. New York: Oxford University Press, pp. 23–44.

Bremner, R. (ed.). 1970–71. *Children and Youth in America* (vol. 1, 1600–1865; vol. 2, 1865–1965). Cambridge, Mass.: Harvard University Press.

Briar, S. 1963. Clinical judgment in foster care placement. *Child Welfare* 42:161–69.

Brown, K., and J. Sunshine. 1982. Group treatment of children from alcoholic families. *Social Work with Groups* 5(1):65–72.

Bryce, M. E., and R. C. Ehlert. 1971. 144 foster children. *Child Welfare* 50(9):499–503.

Burt, M. R., and R. R. Balyeat. 1977. *A Comprehensive Emergency System for Neglected and Abused Children*. New York: Vantage Press.

Burt, M. R., and L. H. Blair. 1971. *Options for Improving Care of Neglected and Dependent Children*. Washington, D.C.: Urban Institute.

Bush, M. 1984. The public and private purposes of case records. *Children and Youth Services Review* 6:1–18.

Canning, R. 1974. School experiences of foster parenting. *Child Welfare* 53:582–87.

Cautley, P. W., and M. J. Aldridge. 1973. *Predictors of Success in Foster Care*. Madison: Wisconsin Department of Health and Social Services.

Chamberlain, P., S. Moreland, and K. Reid. 1992. Enhanced services and stipends for foster parents: Effects on retention rates and outcomes for children. *Child Welfare* 71(5):387–401.

Chernoff, R., R. Combs-Orme, C. Risley-Curtiss, and A. Heisler. 1994. Assessing the health status of children entering foster care. *Pediatrics* 93(4):594–601.

Committee on Ways and Means, U.S. House of Representatives. 1996. *1996 Green Book*. Washington, D.C.: U.S. Government Printing Office.

Cornish, J., and K. Nelson. 1991. Families helping families. *Community Alternatives* 3(2):59–73.

Costin, L., H. J. Karger, and D. Stoesz. 1996. *The Politics of Child Abuse in America.* New York: Oxford University Press.

Courtney, M. 1994a. "Factors Associated with Entry to Group Care." In R. P. Barth, J. D. Berrick, and N. Gilbert (eds.), *Child Welfare Research Review,* vol. 1. New York: Columbia University Press.

Courtney, M. E. 1994b. Factors associated with the reunification of foster children with their families. *Social Service Review* 68:81–108.

Courtney, M. E., R. P. Barth, J. D. Berrick, D. Brooks, R. Needell, and L. Park. 1996. Race and child welfare services: Past research and future directions. *Child Welfare* 75(2):99–138.

Cryns, A., K. Gorey, and G. Brice. 1989. Long-Term Care Outcome Research as a Function of Researcher Location: A Comparative Analysis. Paper presented at the 42nd annual scientific meeting of the Geronotological Society of America, Minneapolis.

Daly, D. L., and T. P. Dowd. 1992. Characteristics of effective, harm-free environments for children in out-of-home care. *Child Welfare* 71(6):487–96.

Danziger, S., Sandefur, G., and Weinberg, D. (eds.). 1994. *Confronting Poverty: Prescriptions for Change.* Cambridge, Mass.: Harvard University Press.

Daro, D. 1988. *Confronting Child Abuse.* New York: The Free Press.

Davis, I. P., J. Landsverk, R. Newton, and W. Ganger. 1996. Parental visiting and foster care reunification. *Children and Youth Services Review* 18(4/5):363–82.

Davis, R. B., P. D. Johnston, L. DiCicco, and A. Orenstein. 1985. Helping children of alcoholic parents: An elementary school program. *School Counselor* 32(5):357–63.

DiCicco, L., R. Biron, J. Carifio, C. Deutsch, D. J. Mills, A. Orenstein, A. Re, H. Unterberger, and R. E. White. 1984. Evaluation of the CASPAR alcohol education curriculum. *Journal of Studies on Alcohol* 45(2):160–69.

DiCicco, L., R. Davis, and A. Orenstein. 1984. Identifying the children of alcoholic parents from survey responses. *Journal of Alcohol and Drug Education* 30(1):1–17.

Donnelly, B. P. 1980. *A Policy Review of California's Foster Care Placement and Payment Systems.* Report No. S80-6 (May 1980). State of California, Department of Finance, Program Evaluation Unit.

Dore, M. M., T. M. Young, and D. M. Pappenfort 1984. Comparison of basic data for the national survey of residential group care facilities: 1966–1982. *Child Welfare* 36(6):485–95.

Downs, S. W. 1986. Black foster parents and agencies: Results of an eight state survey. *Children and Youth Services Review* 8:201–18.

Dubowitz, H., S. Feigelman, D. Harrington, R. Starr, Jr., S. Zuravin, and R. Sawyer. 1994. Children in kinship care: How do they fare? *Children and Youth Services Review* 16(1/2):85–106.

Dubowitz, H., S. Feigelman, and S. Zuravin. 1993. A profile of kinship care. *Child Welfare* 72(2):153–69.

Dumaret, A. 1985. IQ, scholastic performance and behavior of sibs raised in contrasting environments. *Journal of Child Psychology and Psychiatry* 26:553–80.

Edin, K. 1995. Single mothers and child support: The possibilities and limits of child support policy. *Children and Youth Services Review* 17(1/2):203–30.

Edin, K. and L. Lien. 1997. *Making Ends Meet: How Single Mothers Survive Welfare and Low-Wage Work.* New York: Russell Sage Foundation.

Ellwood, D. T. 1986. "Targeting Would-Be Long Recipients of AFDC" prepared for the U.S. Department of Health and Human Services by Mathematica Policy Research.

Ellwood, D. T., and M. J. Bane. 1985. "The Impact of AFDC on Family Structure and Living Arrangements." In R. G. Ehrenberg (ed.), *Research in Labor Economics,* vol. 7. Greenwich, Conn.: JAI Press.

Emlen, A., J. Lahti, G. Downs, A. McKay, and S. Downs. 1977. *Overcoming Barriers to Planning for Children in Foster Care.* Portland, Ore.: Regional Research Institute for Human Services, Portland State University.

Emlen, A., J. Lahti, G. Downs, A. McKay, and S. Downs. 1978. *Overcoming Barriers to Planning for Children in Foster Care.* DHEW Publication No. (OHDS) 78-30138. Washington, D.C.: U.S. Department of Health and Human Services, U.S. Children's Bureau.

Emlen, A., J. Lahti, K. Liedtke, and G. Downs. 1976. *Barriers to Planning for Children in Foster Care.* Portland, Ore.: Regional Research Institute for Human Services, Portland State University.

Epstein, W. M. 1984a. Technology and social work 1: The effectiveness of psychotherapy. *Journal of Applied Social Sciences* 8(2):155–75.

Epstein, W. M. 1984b. Technology and social work 2: Psychotherapy, family therapy, and implications for practice." *Journal of Applied Social Sciences* 8(2):175–87.

Epstein, W. M. 1993a. *The Dilemma of American Social Welfare.* New Brunswick, N.J.: Transaction Publishers.

Epstein, W. M. 1993b. Randomized controlled trials in the human services. *Social Work Research and Abstracts,* September, pp. 3–10.

Epstein, W. M. 1995. *The Illusion of Psychotherapy.* New Brunswick, N.J.: Transaction Publishers.

Epstein, W. M. 1997. *Welfare in America: How Social Science Fails the Poor.* Madison: University of Wisconsin Press.

Everett, J. E., S. S. Chipungu, and B. R. Leashore. 1991. *Child Welfare: An Africentric Perspective.* New Brunswick, N.J.: Rutgers University Press.

Fanshel, D. 1976. Status changes of children in foster care: Final results of the Columbia University longitudinal study. *Child Welfare* 55:143–71.

Fanshel, D. 1979. Preschoolers entering foster care in New York City: The need to stress plans for permanency. *Child Welfare* 58:67–87.

Fanshel, D., S. Finch, and J. Grundy. 1989. Modes of exit from foster family care and adjustment at time of departure of children with unstable life histories. *Child Welfare* 68(4):391–401.

Fanshel, D., and E. Shinn. 1978. *Children in Foster Care: A Longitudinal Investigation.* New York: Columbia University Press.

Fein, E., and A. N. Maluccio. 1984. Children leaving foster care: Outcomes of permanency planning. *Child Abuse and Neglect* 8:425–31.

Fein, E., A. N. Maluccio, V. J. Hamilton, and D. E. Ward. 1983. After foster care: Permanency planning for children. *Child Welfare* 62(6):485–558.

Fein, E., A. N. Maluccio, and M. P. Kluger. 1990. *No More Partings: An Examination of Long-term Foster Family Care.* Washington, D.C.: Child Welfare League of America.

Fein, E., and I. Staff. 1991. Implementing reunification services. *Families in Society* 42:335–43.

Fein, E., and I. Staff. 1993. Last best chance: Findings from a reunification services program. *Child Welfare* 72:25–40.

Feldman, L. H. 1990. *Evaluating the Impact of Family Preservation Services in New Jersey.* Trenton: New Jersey Division of Youth and Family Services, Bureau of Research, Evaluation and Quality Assurance.

Ferguson, T. 1966. *Children in Care—and After.* London: Oxford University Press.

Festinger, T. 1983. *No One Ever Asked Us: A Postscript to Foster Care.* New York: Columbia University Press.

Festinger, T. 1996. Going home and returning to foster care. *Children and Youth Services Review* 18(4/5):383–402.

Fields, S. 1975. The children's hour: I. Parents as therapists. *Innovations* 2(3):3–8.

Finch, S., D. Fanshel, and J. Grundy. 1986. Factors associated with the discharge of children from foster care. *Social Work Research and Abstracts* 22(1):10–18.

Fischer, J. 1973a. Has Mighty Casework struck out? *Social Work* 18(4):107–10.

Fischer, J. 1973b. Is casework effective: A review. *Social Work* 18(1):5–20.

Fischer, J. 1981. The social work revolution. *Social Work* 26(3):199–209.

Fitzgerald, M. T., and R. M. Fischer. 1987. A family involvement model for hearing-impaired infants. *Topics in Language Disorders* 7(3):1–18.

Fitzgerald, M. T., and D. E. Karnes. 1987. A parent-implemented language model for at-risk and developmentally delayed preschool children. *Topics in Language Disorders* 7(3):31–46.

Fitzharris, T. 1985. *The Foster Children of California: Profiles of 10,000 Children in Residential Care.* Sacramento, Calif.: Children's Services Foundation.

Fleiss, J. H. 1986. *The Design and Analysis of Clinical Experiments.* New York: Wiley.

Fox, M., and K. Arcuri. 1980. Cognitive and academic functioning in foster children. *Child Welfare* 59(8):491–96.

Frank, G. 1980. Treatment needs of children in foster care. *American Journal of Orthopsychiatry* 50(2):256–63.

Fraser, M. W., P. J. Pecora, and D. A. Haapala. 1991. *Families in Crisis: The Impact of Intensive Family Preservation Services.* New York: Aldine de Gruyter.

Fraser, M. W., E. Walton, R. E. Lewis, P. J. Pecora, and W. K. Walton. 1996. An experiment in family reunification: Correlates of outcomes at one-year follow-up. *Children and Youth Services Review* 18:335–62.

Galaway, B., R. W. Nutter, and J. Hudson. 1995. Relationship between discharge outcomes for treatment foster-care clients and program characteristics. *Journal of Emotional and Behavioral Disorders* 3(1):46–54.

Gans, H. J. 1995. *The War against the Poor.* New York: Basic Books.

GAO (U.S. General Accounting Office). 1989. *Foster Parents: Recruiting and Pre-*

service Training Practices Need Evaluation. GAO/HRD-89-86. Washington, D.C.: Author.

Gaudin, J. M. Jr., and H. Dubowitz. 1997. "Family Functioning in Neglectful Families: Recent Research." In J. D. Berrick, R. Barth, and N. Gilbert (eds.), *Child Welfare Research Review*, vol. 2. New York: Columbia University Press.

Gelles, R. J. 1996. *The Book of David: How Preserving Families Can Cost Children's Lives.* New York: Basic Books.

Gelles, R. J., and M. A. Straus. 1988. *Intimate Violence.* New York: Simon and Schuster.

Gil, D. 1970. *Violence against Children.* Cambridge, Mass.: Harvard University Press.

Gilbert, N., and H. Specht. 1978. "Introduction." In T. J. Stein, E. D. Gambrill, and K. T. Wiltse (eds.), *Children in Foster Homes: Achieving Continuity of Care.* New York: Praeger.

Glisson, C. 1996. Judicial and service decisions for children entering state custody: The limited role of mental health. *Social Service Review* 70:257–81.

Goerge, R. M. 1990. The reunification process in substitute care. *Social Service Review* 64:422–57.

Goerge, R. M. 1993. *Special Education Experiences of Foster Children: An Emperical Study.* Chicago: University of Chicago, Chapin Hall Center for the Study of Children.

Goerge, R. M. 1994. "The Effect of Public Child Welfare Worker Characteristics and Turnover on Discharge from Foster Care." In R. P. Barth, J. D. Berrick, and N. Gilbert (eds.), *Child Welfare Research Review*, vol. 1. New York: Columbia University Press.

Gordon, L. 1988. *Heroes of Their Own Lives: The Politics and History of Family Violence, Boston 1880–1960.* New York: Penguin Books.

Gorey, K. M. 1996. Effectiveness of social work intervention research: Internal versus external evaluations. *Social Work Research* 20(2):119–28.

Gruber, A. R. 1978. *Children in Foster Care: Destitute, Neglected, Betrayed.* New York: Human Sciences Press.

Halfon, N., G. Berkowitz, and L. Klee. 1992. Mental health service utilization by children in foster care in California. *Pediatrics* 89(6):1238–44.

Halfon, N., A. Mendonca, and G. Berkowitz. 1995. Health status of children in foster care: The experience of the Center of the Vulnerable Child. *Archives of Pediatrics and Adolescent Medicine* 149:386–92.

Halper, G., and M. A. Jones. 1981. *Serving Families at Risk of Dissolution: Public Preventive Services in New York City.* New York: Human Resources Administration.

Haskell, T. L. 1996. "Justifying the Rights of Academic Freedom." In L. Menand (ed.), *The Future of Academic Freedom.* Chicago: University of Chicago Press.

Haynes, C., C. Culter, J. Gray, J. O'Keefe, and R. Kemps. 1983. Non-organic failure to thrive: Implication of placement through analysis of video-taped interactions. *Child Abuse and Neglect* 7:321–28.

Hernandez, D. J. 1993. *America's Children: Resources from Family, Government, and the Economy.* New York: Russell Sage.

Hester, P. 1977. Evaluation and accountability in a parent-implemented early intervention service. *Community Mental Health Journal* 13(3):261–67.

Hester, P., and J. Hendrickson. 1977. Training functional expressive language: The acquistion and generalization of five-element syntactic responses. *Journal of Applied Behavior Analysis* 10(2):316.

Hochstadt, N., P. Jaudes, D. Zimo, and J. Schachter. 1987. The medical and psychosocial needs of children entering foster care. *Child Abuse and Neglect* 11:53–62.

Hulsey, T., and R. White. 1989. Family characteristics and measures of behavior in foster and nonfoster children. *American Journal of Orthopsychiatry* 59(4):502–9.

Jenkins, S. 1967. Duration of foster care: Some relevant antecedent variables. *Child Welfare* 46(8):450–55.

Jeter, H. R. 1963. *Children, Problems, and Services in Child Welfare Programs*. Washington, D.C.: Children's Bureau.

Joint Commission on Mental Health of Children. 1973. *The Mental Health of Children: Services, Research, and Manpower*. New York: Harper and Row.

Jones, M. A. 1985. *A Second Chance for Families: Five Years Later*. New York: Child Welfare League of America.

Jones, M. A., R. Neuman, and A. Shyne. 1976. *A Second Chance for Families: Evaluation of a Program to Reduce Foster Care*. New York: Child Welfare League of America.

Journal of the American Medical Association. 1997. "Applying Science to Violence Prevention." 277(20):1641–42.

Kadushin, A. 1974. *Child Welfare Services*. New York: Macmillan.

Kaplun, D., and R. Reich. 1976. The murdered child and his killers. *American Journal of Psychiatry* 133:809–13.

Kempe, C. H., F. N. Silverman, B. F. Steele, W. Droegemueller, and H. K. Silver. 1962, July. The battered child syndrome. *Journal of the American Medical Association* 181:17–24.

Kennedy, J. F., and V. T. Keeney. 1987. Group psychotherapy with grandparents rearing their emotionally disturbed grandchildren. *Group* 1 (spring):15–25.

Kent, J. T. 1976. A follow-up study of abused children. *Journal of Pediatric Psychology* 1:25–31.

Kinard, E. M. 1982. Experiencing child abuse: Effects on emotional adjustment. *American Journal of Orthopsychiatry* 52:82–91.

Kinney, J., D. Haapala, C. Booth, and S. Leavitt. 1988. "The Homebuilders Model." In J. K. Whittaker, T. Kinney, E. M. Tracy, and C. Booth (eds.), *Reaching High-Risk Families: Intensive Family Preservation Services*. New York: Aldine de Gruyter.

Kirst, M., and M. Wald. 1989. *Conditions of Children in California*. Berkeley: Policy Analysis for California Education.

Klee, L., and N. Halfon. 1987. Mental health care for foster children in California. *Child Abuse and Neglect* 15(1):63–74.

Knitzer, J. 1982. *Unclaimed Children: The Failure of Public Responsibility to Children and Adolescents in Need of Mental Health Services*. Washington, D.C.: Children's Defense Fund.

Knitzer, J., M. L. Allen, and B. McGowan. 1978. *Children without Homes: An Examination of Public Responsibility to Children in Out-of-Home Care.* Washington, D.C.: Children's Defense Fund.

Knudsen, D. D. 1988. *Child Services: Discretion, Decisions, Dilemmas.* Springfield, Ill.: Charles C. Thomas.

Koontz, D. 1981. *The Mask.* New York: Berkley Books.

Kosinski, J. 1965. *The Painted Bird.* Boston: Houghton Mifflin.

Kutash, K., and V. R. Rivera. 1995. Effectiveness of children's mental health services: a review of the literature. *Education and Treatment of Children* 18(4):443–77.

Lahti, J. 1982. A follow-up study of foster children in permanent placements. *Social Service Review* (4):556–71.

Lahti, J., K. Green, A. C. Emlen, J. Zadny, Q. D. Clarkson, M. Kuehnel, and J. Casciato. 1978. *A Follow-up Study of the Oregon Project.* Portland, Ore.: Portland State University, Regional Research Institute for Human Services, School of Social Work.

Lambert, M. J., D. A. Shapiro, and A. E. Bergin. 1986. "The Effectiveness of Psychotherapy." In S. L. Garfiel and A. E. Bergin (eds.), *Handbook of Psychotherapy and Behavior Change.* New York: Wiley.

Lawder, E. A., J. E. Poulin, and R. G. Andrews. 1986. A study of 185 foster children five years after placement. *Child Welfare* 65(3):241–51.

Leitenberg, H., J. D. Burchard, D. Healy, and E. J. Fuller. 1981. Nondelinquent children in state custody: Does type of placement matter? *American Journal of Community Psychology* 9(3):347–60.

Lerman, P. 1975. *Community Treatment and Social Control: A Critical Analysis of Juvenile Correctional Policy.* Chicago: University of Chicago Press.

Levison, C. 1982. Remediating a passive aggressive emotionally disturbed preadolescent boy through writing: A comprehensive psychodynamic structured approach. *Pointer* 26(2):23–27.

Lindhom, B. W., and J. Touliatos. 1978. Characteristics of foster families. *Social Thought* 1(4):45–56.

Lindsey, D. 1991. Factors affecting the foster care placement decision: An analysis of national survey data. *American Journal of Orthopsychiatry* 61(2):272–81.

Lindsey, D. 1992. Adequacy of income and the foster care placement decision: Using an odds ratio approach to examine client variables. *Social Work Research and Abstracts* 28(3):29–36.

Lindsey, D. 1994. *The Welfare of Children.* New York: Oxford University Press.

Linnihan, P. C. 1977. Adolescent day treatment: A community alternative to institutionalization of the emotionally disturbed adolescent. *American Journal of Orthopsychiatry* 47(4):679–88.

Littner, N. 1974. *Some Traumatic Effects of Separation and Placement.* New York: Child Welfare League of America.

Luborsky, L., B. Singer, and L. Luborsky. 1975. Comparative studies of psychotherapies: Is it true that "everybody has won and all must have prizes"? *Archives of General Psychiatry* 32:995–1008.

Lyle, C. G., and J. Nelson. 1983. *Home Based vs. Traditional Child Protection Services: A Study of the Home Based Services Demonstration Project in the Ramsey County Community Human Services Department.* Unpublished paper. St. Paul, Minn.: Ramsey County Community Human Services Department.

Maas, H. S. 1969. Children in long-term foster care. *Child Welfare* 48:321–33.

Maas, H. S., and R. E. Engler Jr. 1959. *Children in Need of Parents.* New York: Columbia University Press.

Magura, S. 1979. Trend analysis in foster care. *Social Work Research and Abstracts* 18:29–36.

Magura, S. 1981. Are services to prevent foster care effective? *Children and Youth Services Review* 3:193–212.

Martinson, R. 1974. What works—Questions and answers about prison reform. *Public Interest,* spring, pp. 22–54.

Mayer, S. E. 1997. *What Money Can't Buy.* Cambridge: Harvard University Press.

Maza, P. 1983. Characteristics of children in foster care. *Child Welfare Research Notes* 1:1–6.

McCord, J. 1983. A forty year perspective on effects of child abuse and neglect. *Child Abuse and Neglect* 7:265–70.

McDonald, W. R., and Associates. 1990. *Evaluation of AB 1562 In-Home Care Demonstration Projects: Final Report.* Sacramento, Calif.: Author.

McIntyre, A., and T. Y. Keesler. 1986. Psychological disorders among foster children. *Journal of Clinical Child Psychology* 15(4):297–303.

McMurtry, S. L., and G. W. Lie. 1992. Differential exit rates of minority children in foster care. *Social Work Research and Abstracts* 28(1):42–48.

Mech, E. V. 1983. Out-of-home placement rates. *Social Service Review* 57(4):659–67.

Meezen, W., and J. McCroskey. 1996. Improving family functioning through family preservation services: Results of the Los Angeles Experiment. *Family Preservation Journal* 1:9–30.

Meier, E. G. 1965. Current circumstances of former foster children. *Child Welfare* 44:196–206.

Meinert, C. L. 1986. *Clinical Trials: Design, Conduct, and Analysis.* Oxford: Oxford University Press.

Menand, L. 1997a. How to frighten small children. *New Yorker,* October 6, pp. 112–13.

Menand, L. 1997b. Inside the Billway. *New York Review of Books.* August 14, pp. 4–7.

Mnookin, R. H. 1973. Foster care—In whose best interest? *Harvard Educational Review* 43:599–638.

Moffitt, R. 1992. Incentive effects of the US welfare system: a review. *Journal of Economic Literature* 30:1–61.

Oates, J. C. 1998. "A lost generation." *New York Review of Books.* July 16, pp. 12–14.

O'Brien, N., T. McClellan, and D. Alf. 1992. Data collection: Are social workers reliable? *Administration in Social Work* 16(2):89–99.

Palmer, S. E. 1979. Predicting outcomes in long-term foster care. *Journal of Social Service Research* 3:201–14.

Pardek, J. T. 1984. *The Forgotten Children: A Study of Stability and Continuity of Foster Care*. Washington, D.C.: University Press of America.

Parrish, V., and P. Hester. 1980. Controlling behavioral techniques in an early intervention program. *Community Mental Health Journal* 16(2):169–75.

Pasztor, E. M. 1985. Permanency planning and foster parenting: Implications for recruitment, selection, training, and retention. *Children and Youth Services Review* 7:191–205.

Pecora, P. J., M. W. Fraser, and D. A. Haapala. 1992. Intensive home-based services: An update from the FIT project. *Child Welfare* 71:177–87.

Pecora, P. J., M. W. Fraser, K. E. Nelson, J. McCroskey, and W. Meezen. 1995. *Evaluating Family-Based Services*. New York: Aldine de Gruyter.

Pecora, P. J., J. K. Whittaker, and A. N. Maluccio (eds.). 1992. *The Child Welfare Challenge: Policy, Practice, and Research*. New York: Aldine de Gruyter.

Pelton, L. 1989. *For Reasons of Poverty: A Critical Analysis of the American Child Welfare System*. Westport, Conn.: Praeger.

Pelton, L. 1994. "The Role of Material Factors in Child Abuse and Neglect." In B. B. Melton and F. D. Barry (eds.), *Protecting Children from Abuse and Neglect: Foundations for a New National Strategy*. New York: Guilford Press.

Pelton, L. (ed.). 1981. *The Social Context of Child Abuse and Neglect*. New York: Human Sciences Press.

Phillips, M. H., B. L. Haring, and A. W. Shyne. 1972. *A Model for Intake Decisions in Child Welfare*. New York: Child Welfare League of America.

Phillips, M. H., A. W. Shyne, and B. L. Haring. 1971. *Factors Associated with Placement Decisions in Child Welfare*. New York: Child Welfare League of America.

Pike, V. 1976. Permanent planning for foster care: The Oregon Project. *Children Today* 5:22–25.

Pine, B. A., R. Warsh, and A. N. Maluccio (eds.). 1993. *Together Again: Family Reunification in Foster Care*. Washington, D.C.: Child Welfare League of America.

Rainwater, L., and T. M. Smeeding. 1995. *Doing Poorly: The Real Income of American Children in a Comparative Perspective*. Syracuse, N.Y.: Syracuse University, Maxwell School.

Rank, M. R. 1994. *Living on the Edge: The Realities of Welfare in America*. New York: Columbia University Press.

Regional Intervention Program. 1976. A parent-implemented early intervention program for preschool children. *Hospital and Community Psychiatry* 27(10):728–31.

Reid, W. J., and P. Hanrahan. 1982. Recent evaluations of social work: Grounds for optimism. *Social Work* 27(4):328–40.

Reid, W., R. Kagan, and S. Schlossberg. 1988. Prevention of placement: Critical factors in program success. *Child Welfare* 67:25–36.

Resnick, G., and M. R. Burt. 1996. Youth at risk: Definitions and implications for service delivery. *American Journal of Orthopsychiatry* 66(2):172–88.

Rest, E. R., and K. W. Watson. 1984. Growing up in foster care. *Child Welfare* 62:291–306.

Risley-Curtiss, C., R. Combs-Orme, R. Chernoff, and A. Heisler. 1996. Health care utilization by children entering foster care. *Research on Social Work Practice* 6(4):442–61.

Rogers, S., and A. Leunes. 1979. A psychometric and behavioral comparison of delinquents who were abused as children and their non-abused peers. *Journal of Clinical Psychology* 35:470–72.

Rossi, P. H. 1991. *Evaluating Family Preservation Programs: A Report to the Edna McConnell Clark Foundation* (mimeograph). New York: Edna McConnell Clark Foundation.

Rossi, P. H. 1994. Book review of "Families in Crisis." *Children and Youth Services Review* 16(5/6):461–65.

Rowe, D. C. 1976. Notes on policy and practice: Attitudes, social class, and the quality of foster care. *Social Service Review* 50(3):506–14.

Rubin, A. 1985. Practice effectiveness: More grounds for optimism. *Social Work* 30:469–76.

Runyan, D. K., and C. L. Gould. 1985. Foster care for child maltreatment: II. Impact on school performance. *Pediatrics* 76:841–47.

Rybczynski, W. 1998. The fifth city. *New York Review of Books*. February 5, pp. 12–18.

Rzepnicki, T. L. 1987. Recidivism of foster children returned to their own homes: A review and new directions for research. *Social Service Review* 61(1):56–70.

Rzepnicki, T. L., J. R. Schuerman, and P. R. Johnson. 1997. "Facing Uncertainty: Reuniting High-Risk Families." In J. D. Berrick, R. Barth, and N. Gilbert (eds.), *Child Welfare Research Review*, vol. 2. New York: Columbia University Press.

Schaeffer, M. H., G. W. Kliman, M. J. Friedman, and B. G. Pasquariella. 1981. Children in foster care: A preventive service and research program for a high risk population. *Journal of Preventive Psychiatry* 1(1):47–56.

Schor, E. L. 1982. The foster care system and health status of foster children. *Pediatrics* 69(5):521–28.

Schuerman, J. R., T. L. Rzepnicki, and J. H. Littell. 1994. *Putting Families First: An Experiment in Family Preservation*. New York: Aldine de Gruyter.

Seaberg, J. R., and E. S. Tolley. 1986. Predictors of the length of stay in foster care. *Social Work Research and Abstracts* 22:11–17.

Segal, S. P. 1972. Research on the outcomes of social work therapeutic interventions: A review of the literature. *Journal of Health and Social Behavior* 13:3–17.

Sheldon, B. 1986. Social work effectiveness experiments: Review and implications. *British Journal of Social Work* 16(2):223–42.

Sherman, E. A., R. Neuman, and A. W. Shyne. 1973. *Children Adrift in Foster Care: A Study of Alternative Approaches*. Washington, D.C.: Child Welfare League of America.

Shyne, A. W., and A. G. Schroeder. 1978. *National Study of Social Services to Children and Their Families*. Washington, D.C.: U.S. Children's Bureau.

Simms, M. D., and S. M. Horwitz. 1996. Foster home environments: A preliminary report. *Developmental and Behavioral Pediatrics* 17(3):170–75.

Simon, R. D., and D. K. Simon. 1982. The effect of foster parent selection and training on service delivery. *Child Welfare* 62(8):515–24.

Small, R., K. Kennedy, and B. Bender. 1991. Critical issues for practice in residential treatment: The view from within. *American Journal of Orthopsychiatry* 61(3):327–38.

Smith, M. L., G. V. Glass, and T. I. Miller. 1980. *The Benefits of Psychotherapy.* Baltimore: Johns Hopkins Press.

Stein, E., B. Evans, R. Mazumdar, and N. Rae-Grant. 1996. The mental health of children in foster care: A comparison with community and clinical samples." *Canadian Journal of Psychiatry* 41(6):385–91.

Stein, E., N. Rae-Grant, S. Ackland, and W. Avison. 1994. Psychiatric disorders of children "in care": Methodology and demographic correlates. *Canadian Journal of Psychiatry* 39(6):341–47.

Stein, T. J., and E. D. Gambrill. 1985. Permanency planning for children: The past and present. *Children and Youth Services Review* 7:83–94.

Stein, T. J., E. D. Gambrill, and K. T. Wiltse (eds.). 1978. *Children in Foster Homes: Achieving Continuity of Care.* New York: Praeger.

Stein, T. J., and Rzepnicki, T. L. 1983. "Decision Making in Child Welfare: Current Issues and Future Directions." In B. McGowan and W. Meezen (eds.), *Child Welfare: Current Dilemmas—Future Directions.* Itasca, Ill.: F. E. Peacock, pp. 259–94.

Strain, P. S., P. Steele, T. Ellis, and M. A. Timm. 1982. Long-term effects of oppositional child treatment with mothers as therapists and therapist trainers. *Journal of Applied Behavior Analysis* 15(1):163–69.

Swire, M. R., and F. Kavaler. 1979. The health status of foster children. *Child Welfare* 56:635–53.

Szykula, S. A., and M. J. Fleischman. 1985. Reducing out-of-home placements of abused children: Two controlled field studies. *Child Abuse and Neglect* 9(2): 277–83.

Tatara, T. 1993. *U.S. Child Substitute Care Flow Data for FY '92 and Current Trends in the State Child Substitute Care Populations.* VCIS Research Notes 9 (August). Washington, D.C.: Voluntary Cooperative Information System, American Public Welfare Association.

Tatara, T. 1994. "Some Additional Explanations for the Recent Rise in the U.S. Child Substitute Care Population: An Analysis of National Child Substitute Care Flow Data and Future Research Questions." In R. Barth, J. D. Berrick, and N. Gilbert (eds.), *Child Welfare Research Review,* vol. 1. New York: Columbia University Press.

Testa, M. 1985. *Using Proportional Hazards Models to Measure Progress toward Achieving Permanence after Foster Placement.* Prepared for the American Association of Public Welfare Information Systems Management Conference, Austin, Tex.

Theis, S. 1924. *How Foster Children Turn Out.* New York: State Charities Aid Association.

Thomlison, R. J. 1984. Something works: Evidence from practice effectiveness studies. *Social Work* 29:51–56.

Thornton, J. L. 1987. An Investigation into the Nature of the Kinship Foster Home. Ph.D. diss. Yeshiva University.

Thornton, J. L. 1991. Permanency planning for children in kinship foster homes. *Child Welfare* 70:593–601.

Timm, M. A., and S. Rule. 1981. RIP: A cost-effective parent-implemented program for young handicapped children. *Early Child Development and Care* 7(2/3): 147–63.

Toth, J. 1997. *Orphans of the Living: Stories of America's Children in Foster Care.* New York: Simon and Schuster.

United States Department of Health and Human Services. 1981. *National Study of the Incidence and Severity of Child Abuse and Neglect.* DHHS Publication No. (OHDS)81-30325. Washington, D.C.: U. S. Department of Health and Human Services.

United States General Accounting Office. 1989. *Children and Youths: About 68,000 Homeless and 186,000 in Shared Housing at Any Given Time.* Washington, D.C.: U.S. Government Printing Office.

Urban Systems Research and Engineering, Inc. 1985. *Evaluation of State Activities with Regard to Adoption Disruptions.* Washington, D.C.: Author.

Vasaly, S. M. 1976. *Foster Care in Five States: A Synthesis and Analysis of Studies from Arizona, California, Iowa, Massachusetts, and Vermont.* Washington, D.C.: U.S. Department of Health, Education, and Welfare.

Videka-Sherman, L. 1988. Meta-analysis of research on social work practice in mental health. *Social Work* 33(4):325–38.

Wadsworth, M. E. J. 1984. "Early Stress and Associations with Adult Health, Behavior, and Parenting." In *Stress and Disability in Childhood* (Colston Papers No. 14, Proceedings of the 34th Symposium of the Colston Research Society). Bristol, England: Butler and Corner.

Wald, M. 1975. State intervention on behalf of "neglected" children: A search for realistic standards. *Stanford Law Review* 27:985–1040.

Wald, M. 1976. State intervention on behalf of "neglected" children: Standards for removal of children from their homes, monitoring the status of children in foster care, and termination of parental rights. *Standford Law Review* 28:625–706.

Wald, M., C. M. Carlsmith, and P. H. Leiderman. 1988. *Protecting Abused and Neglected Children.* Palo Alto, Calif.: Stanford University Press.

Walton, E. 1991. The Reunification of Children with Their Families: A Test of Intensive Family Treatment Following Out-of-Home Placement. Ph.D. diss. University of Utah.

Wells, K. 1993. Residential treatment as long-term treatment: An examination of some issues. *Children and Youth Services Review* 15(3):195–217.

Wells, K., and D. Whittington. 1993. Characteristics of youths referred to residential treatment: Implications for program design. *Children and Youth Services Review* 15(3):195–217.

Weston, J. 1974. "The Pathology of Child Abuse." In R. Helfer and C. H. Kempe (eds.), *The Battered Child.* 2d ed. Chicago: University of Chicago Press.

Widom, C. S. 1994. "The Role of Placement Experiences in Mediating the Criminal Consequences of Early Childhood Victimization." In R. P. Barth, J. D. Berrick, and N. Gilbert (eds.), *Child Welfare Research Review,* vol. 1. New York: Columbia University Press.

Willems, D. N., and R. DeRubeis. 1981. *The Effectiveness of Intensive Preventive Services for Families with Abused, Neglected, or Disturbed Children: Hudson County Project Final Report.* Trenton: Bureau of Research, New Jersey Division of Youth and Family Services.

Wolock, I., and B. Horowitz. 1979. Child maltreatment and material deprivation among AFDC recipient families. *Social Service Review* 53:530–43.

Wood, K. M. 1978. Casework effectiveness: A new look at the research evidence. *Social Work* 23:437–58.

Wood, S., K. Barton, and C. Schroeder. 1988. In-home treatment of abusive families: Cost and placement at one year. *Psychotherapy* 25(3):409–14.

Wootton, B. 1959. *Social Science and Social Pathology.* London: George Allen and Unwin.

Wulczyn, F. H. 1991. Case load dynamics and foster care reentry. *Social Service Review* 65(1):133–56.

Wulczyn, F. H. 1994. "Status at Birth and Infant Foster Care Placements in New York City." In R. P. Barth, J. D. Berrick, and N. Gilbert (eds.), *Child Welfare Research Review*, vol. 1. New York: Columbia University Press.

Wulczyn, F. H., and R. M. Goerge. 1992. Foster care in New York and Illinois: The challenge of rapid change. *Social Service Review* 66(2):278–94.

Wulczyn, F., and D. Zeidman. 1997. "HomeRebuilders: A Family Reunification Demonstration Project." In J. D. Berrick, R. Barth, and N. Gilbert (eds.), *Child Welfare Research Review*, vol. 2. New York: Columbia University Press.

Zuravin, S. J., M. Benedict, and M. Somerfield. 1997. "Child Maltreatment in Family Foster Care: Foster Home Correlates." In J. D. Berrick, R. Barth, and N. Gilbert (eds.) *Child Welfare Research Review*, vol. 2. New York: Columbia University Press.

Index

Structural factors, 33, 38–39, 52, 111, 129–130
Study outcomes. *See* Child welfare literature
Subcultural factors, 39, 129–130
Sunshine, J., 117
Surrogate parents, 119, 123
Survey of Income and Program Participation (SIPP), xv
Swire, M. R., 55
Szykula, S. A., 107

Tatara, T., xvi*n*2, 42, 52*n*11, 52–53, 53*n*12
Testa, M., 45
Theis, S., 71
Therapeutic services. *See* Psychotherapy
Thomlison, R. J., 113
Thornton, J. L., 62
Timm, M. A., 117
Tolley, E. S., 47–48
Toth, J., 74
Touliatos, J., 57
Treatment Foster Care (TFC), 119–120

University of California, Berkeley, 90
University of Chicago, 98–99
Urban Systems Research and Engineering, 64
U.S. Department of Health and Human Services, 61*n*18
U.S. General Accounting Office (GAO), 56–57, 57*n*13, 59, 116, 118
Utah experiment, 96, 101

Vasaly, S. M., 45, 60

Vermont. *See* Casey Family Services (CFS) program
Videka-Sherman, L., 114
Voluntary Cooperative Information System, 53*n*12
Volunteers for Children in Need, 63*n*20

Wadsworth, M. E. J., 55
Wald, M., 44, 55, 65*n*22, 66, 66*n*23, 101
Walton, E., Family Reunification Services (FRS), 97
Warsh, R., 46
Watson, K. W., 55
Weinberg, D., 36
Welfare, xi, 32, 37; reform, 57, 113*n*16
Wells, K., 56
Weston, J., 61*n*18
White, R. B., 46–47, 48*n*8; 55, 67
Whittaker, J. K., family preservation, 106
Whittington, D., 56
Widom, C. S., 67
Willems, D. N., 108
Wiltse, K. T., 66; Alameda experiment, 89–90
Wolock, I., 61*n*18
Wood, K. M., 112, 114
Wood, S., 107
Wootton, B., 112
Wulczyn, F. H., 37, 42, 49, 64; Home-Rebuilders, 99–100

Young, T. M., 64

Zeidman, D., HomeRebuilders, 99–100
Zuravin, S. J., 58, 62–63